The Allotment Experience

Everything you need to know about allotment gardening
– direct from the plot

RUTH BINNEY

SPRING HILL

Published by Spring Hill, an imprint of How To Books Lt
Spring Hill House, Spring Hill Road
Begbroke, Oxford OX5 1RX United Kingdom
Tel: (01865) 375794
Fax: (01865) 379162
info@howtobooks.co.uk
www.howtobooks.co.uk

How To Books greatly reduce the carbon footprint of their books
by sourcing their typesetting and printing in the UK.

The paper used for this book is FSC certified and totally chlorine free. FSC (The Forest Stewardship
Council) is an international network to promote responsible management of the world's forests.

British Library Cataloguing in Publication Data
A catalogue record of this book is available from the British Library

ISBN: 978 1 905862 26 9

Produced for How To Books by Deer Park Productions, Tavistock, Devon
Designed and typeset by Mousemat Design Ltd
Printed and bound by in Great Britain by Bell & Bain Ltd, Glasgow

NOTE: The material contained in this book is set out in good faith for general guidance and no
liability can be accepted for loss or expense incurred as a result of relying in particular circumstances on
statements made in the book. Laws and regulations are complex and liable to change, and readers
should check the current position with relevant authorities before making personal arrangements.

For Paula, who started it all,
and in loving memory of Donald who died
just as this book was going to press.

v

CONTENTS

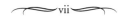

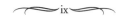

INTRODUCTION

We love our allotment. We love eating the fresh fruit and vegetables we grow and picking sweet peas. We love seeing the buzzard perching on our shed. We even love weeding, though are admittedly less enthusiastic about rabbits and potato blight. We love the idea that we are cutting down our carbon footprint. Most of all we relish the good that the allotment does for us in body and soul, and the friends that we've made on our plots.

In early 1983 my husband Donald celebrated his 50th birthday. It was a time when he was without a permanent job and life was not going well for him. As a gift, a dear friend 'acquired' an allotment for him in Duke's Meadows in Chiswick and soon we were both totally hooked in every way on the 'allotment experience'. As well as giving us the chance to grow our own food (and battle the weeds), tending our plot did wonders for mind and body, and was a welcome refuge from the claustrophobia of flat life. Although we had both gardened before, and I had helped my father on an allotment many years earlier, there was much to learn – from books and, of course, from trial and error. The asparagus there was to die for, and worth the car journey which, on a bad traffic day, could take at least half an hour each way. Our daughter Laura spent many happy hours playing up there, often with friends. Picnics, hosing and bonfires were definitely the main attractions. Now, as an adult, she truly appreciates it:

I think coming to see your allotment was amazing – incredible that so much produce can come from dedicated gardening! (Laura Tucker)

Eight years later we moved to Hampstead and, thanks again to an act of friendship, we took on a big plot in Highgate. This is a magnificent site, once farmland, just behind the golf course and has been an allotment site since 1896. Worth billions in real estate it is, I maintain, even more valuable as land for gardening, relaxation and all the other pleasure that the allotment brings. There we took on committee jobs and got involved in the running of the site, and were happy to do so, swearing that if ever the developers thought of moving in we would be first to the barricades.

For the last six years we have been tending an allotment just outside Dorchester, for although we have a garden at home it is not big enough for proper vegetable growing. However, Donald is still Treasurer of the Highgate Allotment Association and it is excellent to have a reason to keep in touch with all our many friends there. When we left our plot there the waiting list for new ones was 12. It is now 70 plus – tribute indeed to the burgeoning and deserved popularity of allotment gardening, which is now exerting an appeal across an ever broader spectrum.

This book is the result of my own allotment experiences, but also those of the many allotment gardeners who have been so generous with their time, and have given me such excellent quotes to include in this book. It would have been impossible without them and their expertise is reflected throughout the book. In our conversations many themes have recurred – notably the problems of slugs and blight in wet summers such as 2007 when much of this book was being written. It is not intended as a book of 'perfect gardening', far from it. There are many, many allotment gardeners out there with plots streets better than ours. What I hope is that the experiences and advice included will entertain and inspire plot holders old and new (and those on long waiting lists) and, as a result, help to keep the allotment tradition going for the foreseeable future.

A Britain without its allotments would be a poorer place by far, and the same goes for my own life – a thought enhanced by the joy of cooking and eating the produce we grow, although this is not necessarily my thought when I'm picking snails out of a cabbage or find myself making chutney at midnight!

Of all the allotment experiences I have shared in writing this book, I think the poem opposite, written by Esme Scott Hewitt when she was six, sums up the joy of allotments perfectly.

Ruth Binney, West Stafford, Dorset

The Allotment

The Allotment is a place where you grow flowers, fruit and veg.
It is a place where you find secret paths and if you fall over you get muddy.
It is a nice place to run around and ride your bike.
You have a compost heap and bench if you want it.
I like being with my family at the allotment.
My dad mows the lawn, my mum plants everything and I water them.
People are really kind and they help you.

That's WHY I LOVE THE ALLOTMENT!
I love butterflies too!

CHAPTER 1
ALLOTMENT PASSIONS

There is nothing quite like an allotment – it is a very special sort of gardening that for many is highly addictive. So why have one? The answer is for the pure pleasure of growing your own produce – and a lot more besides.

When you step through those gates it's just magical. (Marta Scott)

It's hard work and nothing but. (Damien Grove)

It's food for the soul. (Vicky Scott)

It has a compulsion all of its own – I want to be there all the time. (Ann Tucker)

Growing vegetables, fruit and flowers and enjoying them fresh, tasty and in profusion are the bonus you get for the chance to be outdoors in the fresh air, appreciating nature, taking exercise and getting the soil under your fingernails. The allotment is a haven where you can watch things grow. It may also be the chance you need to have some time completely to yourself. And year by year, through successes and failures, you learn more about gardening.

You can't start taking it in until you start working … until you get your spade in you don't know how to do it. (Marta Scott)

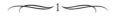

Allotments are classless neighbourhoods where the state of the weather and the soil and the rampaging of rabbits are a million times more important than any gardener's wealth or social standing. An allotment is extra special if you don't have anywhere else to grow things:

Our little patch is just like a garden at home. (Brendan Coffrey)

My boy was a big motivation and as we have no garden I wanted him to be able to get his hands dirty. (Marta Scott)

Some people acquire their allotments almost by accident. The lure of the allotment can then kick in:

We took this over for Tom when he was ill. I have a day off during the week and that's how we began. Now we have another plot of our own down at the far end. (Liz Hanson)

Of course the allotments do involve work, time and some financial outlay. If taking on a plot alone seems too daunting, then you may want to take on one with friends or neighbours, though this may not necessarily work out as you've planned if you don't agree about what you'll grow or can't share out the chores evenly:

We share with our neighbours. We now have a line down the middle. We realized we didn't match but we are still good neighbours. (Liz Hanson)

Even in an 'official' share, you may get to do the biggest load of the work.

There are two couples who officially have the plot I'm on but they don't do much. (Marta Scott)

And you may not agree on how you're going to garden.

We've lost all our lettuces to slugs as the people we share it with don't like using any chemicals. (Angela Franks)

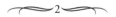

When you're working it can be difficult to fit in all the visits you need to keep the plot as you'd like it, but when you're retired, there is the luxury of regular gardening:

> *I'm at the allotment every day. I'm up there every single morning. I just love being there. It gives a structure to your day. (Maureen Nightingale)*

Allotments are great places for couples and families, although you may not always be able to persuade your children or grandchildren of the advantages of being out in the cold and rain in the middle of winter. Allotments are rescue remedies – for the retired, the redundant, the lonely and the bereaved – because there is good to be had for the soul as well as the body in tending your plot, and friends to be made.

> *My wife died quite suddenly and I'd just retired. I met Bob and he suggested an allotment – it was one of the best things I ever did. Working hard, there wasn't too much time to think. (David Downton)*

> *The sense of community is fantastic when you live in a town rather than a village. (Pat Bence)*

> *He just sits in his armchair and works out his racing schedule and gets the grandchildren working. (Jim Greenhill)*

Or you can even watch the world go by:

> *My first one was in Romsey between a main road and a railway line … it was good for train watching. (Robin Barrett)*

MAKING THE DECISION

Before you take on a plot take some time to think through what it will involve – though if the waiting list is long, your thinking time may stretch to more years than you would wish.

The following are important points to consider.

Location Where are your nearest allotments? If they're not close to home, will you be able to get there and back reasonably easily – and regularly? Will you be snarled up in rush hour traffic if you want to get to the allotment early in the morning or after work?

I have to bike up a hill, then cruise down it on the way home. It's worth it.
(Sue Bryant)

The way you tend your plot will depend a lot on how near it is:

Having the allotment just outside the back gate makes all the difference. You can get on top of silly things like watering which you wouldn't do if it meant taking an hour to go there and back. You can also go out there and tap dance on snails.
(Ken Daniels)

If it means a drive to and fro, you may need to be able to time it neatly.

In London in June and July the mid-week allotment routine was to get back from work by 6.30 or 7.00 at the latest, have a quick snack or pack a picnic supper while the traffic died down, then drive to the allotment for watering and picking. Sometimes we'd see the sun set on Hampstead Heath on the way home, but often it was pitch dark by the time we got back. (Ruth)

Quality Is it a good site? Do the plots look well tended? Is it secluded and secure and likely to be free from thieves and vandals? Sites vary enormously from the well manicured to the scruffy, though if all you want to do is garden, this is going to be immaterial.

You have to ignore the piles of detritus all around (including sheds and plots in progress). I have eyes only for my bit. (Marta Scott)

In selecting this plot (which has its deficiencies) I put some work into the location. I went to the council then went to look at them all and talked to people about the experience they'd had. I was glad I did that. The person I met on this plot was an old boy leaning over the fence. I asked about vandalism and so on.

He told me everything about the plot and the people and in four and a half years I've never heard of vandalism or theft. (Edward Probert)

Does it get plenty of sun? Allotment vegetables are unlikely to thrive in a lot of shade. Is it on a steep slope?

I have a vaguely sloping site angling north that runs east–west. But it drains quite well. (Chris Luck)

Gardening time Do you have the time? An allotment is a big commitment, and the weeds will take over in short order if you're not around to look after your plot. When plants die and the allotment gets messy it's easy to get disheartened and give up. But commitment pays off.

When we go away for a month it's just impossible when we get back. You have to be at it all the time. But we love it. (Brendan Coffrey)

One of the hazards is that it requires one's presence. This particular site is not very well kept up. The plots are very big – we are one of the few that manage to cultivate a whole one. (Anthony Pearson)

If you can only get to your plot a couple of times a week for good long sessions it will still be worthwhile, though you need to be well prepared for the day:

Hot drinks – or comfort things – are essential in the winter. (Marta Scott)

Energy and dedication Do you have the energy? Digging and cultivating an allotment is hard work, and a great way of getting fit, but not necessarily the ideal if you have back problems.

If you are gardening as a couple, one may take the lead:

I do a little labouring, like cutting the grass on my partner's allotments. She has three now and has so much energy … I feel I look like a sloth beside her! (Ron Pankhurst)

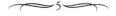

Do you have the commitment? If you love plants and gardening, the answer is bound to be yes, but it's a question worth thinking about.

> *At Highgate, the allotment committee introduced the sensible policy of 'probation', allowing new tenants six months to see if they really were going to be able to tend their plots. If they decided 'no' then they were able to quit straight away with no recriminations and nothing to pay. (Ruth)*

Most council and allotment associations conduct inspections once or twice a year to see whether plots are being properly looked after. If they're not, then they will issue 'dirty plot' warnings and give a deadline by which improvements must be made. This is the point at which you might have to decide whether or not to continue.

Getting an allotment back into shape when you have had an enforced break can be difficult, but worth it.

> *I had to leave the allotment over a long time, but when I came back to it I rescued some crops and I found myself smiling. (Vicky Scott)*

Cost Do you have the money? Renting an allotment is not going to cost a great deal, perhaps up to £50 a year, but you're not necessarily going to save money by growing your own. By the time you've paid for seeds, tools, compost, cloches – and more – the costs can mount up. And there is always the temptation of a water butt, cold frame, greenhouse, a better shed ….

> *You have to spend money. You've got the fresh vegetables but you're paying the price. (Brendan Coffrey)*

The counter argument to this is, of course:

> *I like to grow those things that are expensive to buy – leeks, parsnips and butternut squashes. (Robin Barrett)*

Getting on the waiting list

Allotments are popular and waiting lists are long – and getting longer. This often means that there is pressure to keep plots well tended.

> *Having a waiting list makes the whole site better, I think. (Sue Bryant)*

Even if your name is on the end of a long list there may be ways around the problem. You may be able to join a communal group while you wait, or volunteer to pair up with someone who needs extra help.

> *I started with a group I found on a website – and was a total beginner. They had Sunday afternoon sessions and you could turn up and start learning the works. It's been completely life changing. Then someone I met said they were looking for someone to help them, so I went along and now I have about a third of the plot. I'm aiming for a whole one. I reckon that by the time we get a full-sized plot we'll be ready. (Marta Scott)*

Even when sites seem overgrown and untended, there don't seem to be many vacancies.

> *It's sad that there are so many plots in poor condition. We have 200 plots here and 100 on the waiting list. I think if people don't want them they should put notices up to ask if anyone wants to take them over or share. (Marta Scott)*

Some people get lucky, though:

> *This allotment is larger than I anticipated and I also didn't expect to be told I could take one on straight away. I was a little taken aback. (Ann Tucker)*

If you visit your nearest site and look at the noticeboard, or ask one of the plot holders, you'll find out who to contact, or you can contact the Allotment Association.

> *When we were house hunting in Dorset, we were early for one viewing appointment and happened to pass some allotments, which in itself was a good*

omen. Having bought the house we saw, knowing that its garden would be too small for vegetables, we went straight down to the site, looked at the noticeboard and rang to get ourselves on the waiting list. Only three months later we got the offer we wanted … (Ruth)

Most allotments are owned by local councils, but by no means all. Some are privately owned, others outposts of large estates, and to get one you may have to be patient and inquisitive:

Our allotment is owned by the Burghley Estate. When we arrived in Stamford 14 years ago it was being used by a grandfather and his young grandson. A few years afterwards they left and the plot was abandoned. Some time later someone was discovered sleeping rough in the tumbledown shed. He must have been evicted as a lock was put on the gate. One spring I wrote to the Burghley Estate office enquiring as to what was happening to the allotment and asking if I could use it as a 'wild allotment', that is, largely for the benefit of wildlife. Soon it was 'ours'. (Hendrina Ellis)

Choosing a plot

If you're adopting a plot from someone else, your choice will have already been made for you. Otherwise, when plots are allocated (usually once or twice a year), you may have a selection to choose from. You may be conducted around the allotment site by a committee member (which is also a good opportunity to ask questions about the soil, growing conditions etc.) or left to investigate on your own.

Just because there's a plot available it doesn't mean you should take it if it doesn't seem right. As you're looking around, these are some important things to look for and ask about, firstly about the plot itself.

POSITION, SIZE AND CONDITION

• Where it is sited? Is it next to overhanging trees or a high hedge that may block off the light?

• Is it very exposed to wind and weather?

• How big is it? Traditionally, plots usually come in two sizes, 10 and 5 rods, also called in many places whole and half plots. (A rod is 5 yards 6 inches /4.65 metres; it is also called a pole or perch.)

I say don't take on too much at once. Five poles is enough. Gone are the days of the 40-poler to feed a family. With five you can grow all you need. (Sue Bryant)

I have a slightly bigger plot than is practical. It gets sadly out of control. (Edward Probert)

• How near is it to the water taps or tanks?

We love our allotment, but with hindsight the one next door (which was also vacant but looked weedier) would have been a better choice as it is nearer the tanks from which we have to fill our watering cans. We were lured on a freezing January day by good-looking soil and a strawberry patch. (Ruth)

• Is there easy access for delivering large amounts of compost?

Compost confusion. We had a half load of manure delivered on a dark night, on open ground some way from our plot. A few days later we started moving it, not noticing that another pile had been put nearby. On our next visit we found a rather irate note from another plot holder pinned to our shed complaining that we had been taking his compost. Luckily we managed to solve the dispute amicably. (Ruth)

• How long is it since the plot was last cultivated – and was it well looked after, and for how long, by the previous owner?

When I took the plot on about four and a half years ago, on either side were plots that hadn't been used for several years. All of the unused plots have now been taken on and one near me is now maintained in a distressingly good condition. But they live nearby and are retired and have the time. (Edward Probert)

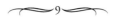

• How weedy is the plot? If very weedy, is it just grass or are there impossibly bad perennial weeds like horsetails? If the latter, say 'no' unless you are very brave, although weeding can be therapeutic:

The weeding is quite something at our allotment. At the end of it all I feel quite human. (Hendrina Ellis)

When we took on our allotment it was completely overgrown – all of it – with no pathways between us and the next allotment. Docks, stinging nettles and millions of brambles. We sprayed it with Roundup [glyphosate] – everything – then it poured with rain for three weeks and we had to do it again. There seemed to be no other way to approach the problem. (Ann Tucker)

• What are the neighbouring plots like? Are they going to blow weed seeds on to yours all the time?

• Does the plot have useful fruit trees, bushes or plants you'd like to keep?

• Is there a shed and, if so, in what condition? Are sheds allowed? Could you have a greenhouse?

THE SITE
These are useful things to know about the site:

• Who owns it? Who manages it? What is the rent and when and to whom is it payable?

• How secure is it? Will you need a key to get in and out? If you lose a key, what is the cost of replacement?

• Is there a separate allotment committee or association and, if so, what are their responsibilities? (They may be delegated by the council to run everything to do with the site.)

• What is the cost of joining and what do you get – is there a club shop or trading post for members selling discount gardening materials – seeds, compost etc.? Does the association have a committee with proper minutes and AGMs?

> *At Highgate we were both on the allotment committee, which met in the communal shed (and 'shop') every couple of months. In winter we would huddle close together on wooden benches to keep warm. Apart from finances we mostly discussed things like problems with trees, deliveries of skips and problems with break-ins, complaints about bonfires and untended plots. One stalwart committee member, who always came with his dog, had been gardening on the site for well over 50 years. (Ruth)*

• Does the site have shows and competitions, parties and barbecues?

• What are the rules about bonfires and the use of weedkillers and pesticides?

• Does the local council or allotment association provide rubbish skips on a regular basis?

• Are working parties organized for big jobs on the site, if these are not done by the council?

> *We have working parties for big jobs such as creosoting the shed and cutting hedges. It's always the same people who turn up. We also need people for carrying deliveries. When you have 120 bags it's hard, and none of us are getting any younger. (Jim Greenhill)*

• Is the site prone to vandals or pests – for instance, is it overrun with rabbits?

• What are the facilities for and rules about car parking? And about dogs, radios and the like?

• Are there any arrangements – formal or informal – for plot sharing?

• Are there any communal places for sitting, for barbecues and so on? Or a play area for children?

• Are there lavatories on the plot or will you have to make do with a bucket in the shed?

• If you wished, would you be allowed to sell your allotment produce?

The communal store

The allotment store, 'shed' or trading post is a wonderful thing if you are lucky enough to have one as it will sell garden supplies bought in bulk and sold at a discount. As well as bags of compost, the best ones will sell things like blood and bone meal, potash, lime and chicken pellets loose and weigh them out for you on the spot. The person who organizes it may also be able to get you tools at good prices and, as well as selling seeds, will order seed potatoes and onion sets every year. Some seed suppliers do special deals with allotment associations, donating a percentage of the price back into the funds.

> I set the shed prices and do all the ordering by phone ... I only took this on temporarily and that was at least six years ago. It means that I do have to be at the shed every Saturday and Sunday but there you go. (Jim Greenhill)

> We had an allotment shop and a newsletter. You could buy plants, seeds, compost, fertilizer. If you really wanted something you could suggest it and they would buy it in for you. (Pat Bence)

As well as the store, someone may also organize exchanges or distribution of excess produce:

> I've got a fruit table to try and distribute to the tenants who haven't got any. (Sue Bryant)

CITY, TOWN AND COUNTRY

The urge to cultivate the land is universal, but allotment gardening is subtly different in town and country. The fact that in urban areas allotment gardeners are less likely to have anywhere else to grow things is reflected in what's grown and in general allotment 'culture'.

If you have no more than a window box, then the allotment is as important for relaxation as it is for digging and growing. Townees undoubtedly keep drinks, mugs and plates in their sheds more often than country allotmenters. And they certainly appreciate their allotments:

Because it's in the town centre, unless you know it's there it's a secret world. (Marta Scott)

In cities and towns, allotment gardeners often live far from their plots, which means that visits are often more extended and less frequent. Country allotments are invariably full of dahlias and gladioli, but they don't have the cottage garden look typical of many town and city allotments.

We've planted a 3-metre square of grass so we can sit out there with a bottle of wine and enjoy the sunset. (Ken Daniels)

In the city, many more allotments have small lawns and decking areas, arbours and all the accoutrements of leisure gardens.

Both our London allotments were almost half an hour away from home, so at weekends we took a picnic and made a day of it, complete with a radio when Test Matches were on. We would brew up on our gas stove, even in winter. In the country, with the allotment just down the road, we do none of these things. We kept deckchairs in the shed to begin with, but after one summer we took them home. (Ruth)

THE ALLOTMENT COMMUNITY

It's the social scene – you meet a lot of people. I keep meeting people who live near me that I don't know. (Vicky Scott)

The best thing about allotments is that it doesn't matter who you are. The one thing you all share is a passion for growing things.

You share plants and cuttings. (Pat Bence)

However, gardeners are very competitive, vying with each other for biggest and best, even if they don't enter their produce in shows. And there is always at least one person who is an 'ace cultivator' (a term coined by the allotment enthusiast Michael Leapman in the column he once wrote for *The Times*).

My next-door allotment holder has the perfect allotment. At first I thought I was going to aim for that, then I realized it was much better to aim for what I could do myself. (Vicky Scott)

As more and more women, couples and young people become interested in gardening, allotment communities are gradually changing from their stereotype of being populated largely by retired 'old codgers'.

Increasingly women are here now which is encouraging. It used to be an all-male preserve. (Chris Luck)

There is plenty of advice on offer, too.

George is my mentor – I feel like a little girl. But he's saved me. I couldn't do without him. (Sue Bryant)

You may also have to deal with the 'know-alls':

When you meet the old buffer who's been doing it for 35 years they tell you you're doing it all wrong. If someone tells me something I believe them – then I try it and make my own mind up. (Ken Daniels)

There is always time for allotment chat – about the weather, the state of weeds and slugs, about the worst and best of what's growing. The allotment is also where you make friends, as well as competing with them to see if you can grow bigger marrows, longer runner beans or superior gladioli.

We've met so many wonderful people on allotments who've lived fascinating lives doing everything from opera singing to park keeping. Our allotment neighbours have given us plants, watered our plot while we've been on holiday and shared our joys and woes. (Ruth)

The oldest chap on our allotments is Eddie who's 85 – he comes on his motorized scooter and is full of advice. (Ann Tucker)

And it's not all work, by any means:

There's a camaraderie about the whole thing – and at the same time an element of competition. You always have a good old chat and end up in the pub. (Mike Cosgrove)

Nor do people always get on:

A couple of elderly people on our plot came to blows with spades – hitting each other – I don't know what it was about. (Chris Luck)

Formalities

Allotment societies vary, but many organize communal events, including barbecues and Christmas parties as well as shows and competitions. If the plots are owned by the council or run by an active association they may carry out annual inspections in late summer and award prizes for the best tended and most varied plots. Or your association may organize regular shows. These are the opportunity to display the best of your produce as well as to learn about the qualities of prize-winning examples, prepared and displayed to RHS standards.

I have just returned from my allotment society awards evening. Needless to say I was not in the running for an award but it was a good social occasion and I had a good chat with the person who was judging the plots. When judging he said that he looked for those growing vegetables and particularly unusual ones. I am trying aubergines this year for the first time. (Andrew Malleson)

INVOLVING YOUR CHILDREN

Allotments are good. I like growing plants and they taste much better. And it's much more peaceful. (Daniel Gittings)

Much as you love your allotment, don't assume that your children will want to spend hours there in foul weather helping you dig and plant.

From my child's perspective we seemed to spend an inordinate amount of time tending the plot. (Liz Palmer)

If your children want to be involved, or even get passionate about the plot, then consider yourself blessed.

We used to take our son in the wheelbarrow – although it was uphill for us. He loved getting dirt on his face. (Richard Harding)

They may even learn something, even if they are too young to know what it means:

When my daughter was little – she was about two – the next-door neighbour asked 'Where have you been?' She said, 'I've been at the allotment learning about photosynthesis.' It's a lovely thing for children. (Vicky Scott)

If they don't want to be involved, then you'll have to find ways of leaving them at home or provide alternative entertainment, which may pay dividends in the long run.

I have an old sandpit for my boy – we bought some new sand. He loves it – it's been his best thing. He takes his toy animals on 'camping trips' to the allotment. He knows a lot of the plant names now and can recognize vegetables. (Marta Scott)

Never let your children run amok on other people's plots. However, they will enjoy exploring, especially if the site has other things on offer.

After the war we rented an allotment on the site of the Ranelagh Club. This former exclusive club, primarily for polo, became derelict with a small part turned into our allotments. I remember exploring the area away from the allotments while my parents dug and planted. The ornate and still impressive pavilion for the polo teams was disintegrating. Nearby was an abandoned open-air swimming pool, with murky water and strange contents. It had a slightly sinister and spooky atmosphere, frightening but strangely magnetic. (Liz Palmer)

On a newly acquired plot, getting children to help make bonfires is fun for all. Stone picking, and hunting for old bits of crockery and other treasure, can also be entertaining. In their initial enthusiasm you will probably also get children to dig, weed and sow seeds of quick-growing vegetables like radishes and lettuce in an area you've designated as their own, though it helps to check out whether they actually like eating the vegetables once they have grown them. On this score, though peas take longer to mature, they can be a much better deal.

He was growing things he liked – onions, garlic, potatoes. Now he couldn't be bothered, but he still helps with things. (Liz Hanson)

When it's cold, a place for kids to sit in a shed is a bonus, and if old enough they may well prefer getting the stove going and making hot drinks to tending the plot. On a hot summer's day, there are few children who won't like watering and hosing (the plants and each other). Barbecues are a great distraction, but for younger ones, pack some toys or games and a couple of picnic rugs. And get their friends to come along for company.

My daughter loves it – now all her friends come down and use all my bean sticks for tepees and play cowboys and Indians. (Vicky Scott)

Harvest time is an ideal opportunity to get children engaged – though for strawberries, raspberries and peas, be prepared for plenty of eating, too. (Pocket money rewards for filled punnets can help reduce losses enormously.) Another good entertainment is scratching initials on a marrow or pumpkin and watching them expand.

Potatoes were my first allotment experience – learning how to rub excess 'chits' off seed potatoes before handing them to my father to put in his trenches. At harvest time it was potato picking for him as he dug, then helping him trundle them home up the hill in the wheelbarrow. (Ruth)

If you take small children to the allotment, a sponge or flannel in a plastic bag for cleaning them up is worth keeping in the shed, along with an old towel.

Keeping the children amused on the plot may even have unexpected results:

When I was at Salisbury in the late sixties I had young children and we used to wander round other allotments and on one was a sty with about six pigs. When I had surpluses like lettuce we used to take them round to the pigs and feed them. We had been doing this for most of one summer – the pigs were happy and we were happy. Then one day the owner was there and was furious. The answer was that he was contracted to Wall's and had to feed the pigs on a specific diet. (Robin Barrett)

PETS

Much as you love your dog, and however much he enjoys accompanying you to the plot, you need to keep the territories and sensibilities of your allotment neighbours in mind. There may even be rules about bringing dogs to the plot, and keeping them on leads. No dog will be welcome that wanders over other people's allotments or even fouls them, nor will one that barks a lot or terrorizes children. If you have any worries about your dog's behaviour, it is best to keep it on a lead, tied to a post or leave it at home.

Many a dog will enjoy dozing in the sun or watching you work and, if you walk to and from the plot, will get exercise into the bargain. It is worth keeping a water bowl in your shed for necessary refreshment.

If you have a problem with a neighbour's dog, try the friendly, polite approach. If this doesn't work you may need to report the problem to your committee.

Plot invasions by neighbouring cats are virtually impossible to control. As well as roaming the allotments, cats will use plots as lavatories and on a sunny day you may even find one asleep among your herbs. On the plus side, feline hunters will help catch rats and mice in and around allotment sheds.

The oddest pets may live at allotments:

Before I took this plot over a nurse had it. She had voles she cultivated almost like pets – they kept eating people's broad beans. Nobody had the heart to tell her about it as she worked in a children's cancer hospital. (David Downton)

THE SHED

Every allotment needs a shed. It's part of the culture – not just for storage. It may even reflect allotment history:

We have some of the quaintest sheds – old railway carriage bits from the Wolverton Works. The old boys would get a bit of railway carriage and make it into a shed. They'd make wooden trucks and carry things in them. (Sue Bryant)

A shed is a distinctive mark of ownership, a place to shelter from the rain, and also provides the essential necessary privacy when you need to change your clothes or pee into a bucket.

My current obsession is having my own shed, so I'm going to put it to the people I share with that I have my own. At the moment I have a secluded 'pee corner' but I need a shed! (Marta Scott)

Allotment sheds range from patched up, ancient and rotting wooden constructions with ramshackle corrugated iron roofs to luxury 'chalets'. If you inherit a shed, it may well come with such deficiencies as leaking sides and wonky roof. Since allotmenters are mostly also conservationists, there's lots of imaginative recycling on view in the average collection of allotment sheds.

Ambitious and thrifty, you may well decide to construct a new shed from scratch.

Skips are wonderful sources of materials and there are sheds around the country made entirely of 'reject' wood gathered from skips. If you need a totally new shed, you may opt for the flat-pack option. But whatever you choose, you need a good base and a construction secure enough that it won't be blown away, lifted up and dumped on your neighbour's plot at the first autumn gale. To help prevent rotting, some kind of preservative is a must (but avoid creosote).

It is worth patching a dodgy roof as soon as you can to keep the rain out, and to batten it down:

Our Highgate shed had a corrugated iron roof – in pieces and loosely attached. In the first gale of the winter large pieces of it flew across the allotment, though luckily didn't damage either people or crops. As a 'temporary measure' (which turned out to be a decade) we found some lumps of concrete and lengths of discarded scaffolding, which we used to keep the roof in place. (Ruth)

A better, more professional solution is to have a shed with a pitched roof, made waterproof with bitumen sheeting or something similar for letting rain run away. This will be better yet if you can attach guttering to allow rainwater to run into an adjacent water butt.

Because security is a burgeoning issue for allotments, some kind of padlock is essential, but unless extremely heavy duty can still get ripped off by vandals or the gangs of thieves who go round allotments taking tools which they later sell off in pubs and at car boot sales. A door that you can secure from the inside is helpful for privacy and shelter. If theft is a real issue on your site you might want to go as far as fitting a burglar alarm, but you will annoy your neighbours if it's so sensitive that it's set off by a passing dog or a strong wind.

It's never advisable to leave expensive tools like strimmers inside the shed. On the one night we did so, the whole plot was 'done over' by a gang, though our strimmer was found next day by our neighbour – thrown into his raspberries. Unfortunately many others on the plot weren't so lucky. On another occasion, an entire shed, newly erected, was stolen, complete with contents. (Ruth)

Windows are an optional extra for the allotment shed and can be plastic or glass. If they don't fit well they can easily get ripped off by the wind and are an obvious entry point for intruders. But nice curtains can greatly enhance a 'posh' shed that's big and tidy enough to eat a meal in.

Assembling your new shed

Though you've bought the flat-pack kit and brought it home, don't be tempted to rush down to the allotment and put it up right away. Physical help and some forethought will pay dividends. You need to wait for a fine day and be sure you have the right tools. And because there's no electricity on allotments you'll need a cordless screwdriver, fully charged up, for the job.

We'd taken the flat pack to the allotment on a blustery day. Despite our best efforts it quickly became obvious that it was going to be impossible to erect it with the puny nails provided. We each tried holding up a side while the other banged in the nails that wouldn't hold and we were getting increasingly frustrated. Then a neighbour from a few plots away approached. 'You'll never do it like that,' he said, in doom-laden tones. 'You need proper screws and an electric screwdriver.' He was so obviously right that we abandoned our task for another day.

Attempt two started well. Two sides were more or less up when the screws we'd bought ran out. So it was suggested that I stood just where I was while Donald 'nipped into town for more screws'. Standing, arms outstretched, for the next 20 minutes was bizarre. But the screws did their job and by the end of the afternoon we had the shed up and the roof on. (Ruth)

What to keep inside

An allotment shed is a bit like a woman's handbag. It contains lots of useful things, but not always in the tidiest arrangement. The number of tools you have can depend on how many people are working the plot, but it usually helps for each person to have their own trowel, fork and spade. Weeding forks, and especially trowels, are extremely personal, with some people favouring a narrow style, others preferring the traditional, wide type.

Since thefts from allotment sheds are increasingly common, the police advise clearly etching or marking your allotment or home postcode on all your tools.

You're likely to be able to find a use for all of the following. Keep any 'chemicals', even organic ones like chicken pellets, out of children's reach.

- Forks, spades and trowels – one per gardener fitted to user size;
- Weeding forks – one or two;
- Hoe – style or styles of your choosing. An onion hoe is an optional extra;
- Rake;
- Dibber;
- Riddle – handy if your ground is very stony, and for sieving compost;
- Secateurs;
- Shears – useful for odd bits of grass edging, though a strimmer is quicker;
- String, labels and pencil;
- Watering cans – two per person if you need them for summer watering;
- Wheelbarrow – though this may need to be kept outside;
- Hose and hose reel – if you have the facility for hosing;
- Buckets or big plastic bins or 'baskets' – for weeds, carrying compost etc.;
- Netting – wide and small mesh. Possibly also very fine 'Enviromesh' for protecting carrots and leeks;
- Collapsible cloches; plastic for polytunnels;
- Fleece and fleece pegs – either the proprietary kind or made yourself from strong wire.

- Chicken pellets;
- Bags of concentrated manure;
- Plant food;
- Bordeaux mixture;
- Insecticide (organic or the alternative);
- Slug pellets;
- Weedkiller – such as glyphosphate.

- Pots for planting. Big ones are handy containers for seedlings when transplanting. They also make handy scoops;

- Scissors – for cutting everything from string and fleece to topping and tailing gooseberries and trimming spring onions;
- Sharp knife – for trimming vegetables and cutting off woody roots;
- Screwdriver – for odd jobs such as tightening a hose attachment;
- Animal-proof container for seed packets;
- Plastic bags – for taking produce home;
- Large plastic sacks (compost empties) – for non-compostable weeds that need to be disposed of;
- Plastic food containers – ideal for harvesting fruit. Those with holes in the base are good for germinating seeds;
- Dustbin – handy for storing apples or potatoes over the winter but must be rodent proof;
- Plastic bottles – cut down to put as guards on tops of sticks and for watering;
- Tissues. Wipes are also handy if you cook and eat at the plot or often have children there;
- Gardening gloves;
- Seasonal gear for all weathers. Plus sunscreen;
- Kneeling pad – to save wear and tear on the joints;
- Mats for sitting and sunbathing;
- Lighter or matches – for bonfires and the gas stove;
- Old newspapers – for bonfire lighting (if allowed) and shredding as soil improvers.

- Bird seed – if you have feeders at your plot and don't mind encouraging the pigeons as well as many beneficial birds.

- Gas stove – size of your choosing, depending on how many picnics you have;
- Tea bags, coffee and sugar in lidded jars. Powdered milk if you wish;
- Mugs;
- Plates and other picnic gear such as knives, forks and spoons;
- Folding chairs.

- Ideally, every shed should contain a first aid kit.

It's easier to keep a shed tidy if you fit it with shelves; old kitchen cupboards make ideal storage units. Hooks and pegs for hanging tools are also a good idea.

In our Highgate shed we inherited an old cupboard complete with shelves which was perfect for storage. It was more solidly built than the shed itself. (Ruth)

If the shed is dark you may be able to improve it:

If you take off the roof panelling and put in Perspex sheeting instead you get more light in so you can grow things. (Sue Bryant)

Shed sharing

You're almost sure to have to share your allotment shed with other living creatures. Mice will take shelter and nest in your shed and have no compunction about chewing through paper so you need to keep seeds – even unopened packets – and foodstuffs like sugar in impenetrable jars.

Much less welcome are rats, which can get in through holes in the shed. Rats are endemic on most city allotments but are attracted to any site where edible scraps have been put on open compost heaps.

Opening the shed door and having a rat run out is a heart-stopping experience. Finding rat droppings around apples you've stored in the open is just plain nasty. (Ruth)

A shed may be a shelter for overwintering butterflies which will flutter out on a sunny spring or winter day. Or birds may treat your shed like a giant nesting box.

One spring we more or less donated our shed to a nesting blackbird but unfortunately the eggs were abandoned before they could hatch. (Ruth)

Be careful what else you keep in your shed.

One weekday evening, about 8.00, someone living near the allotments happened to peer out and saw smoke coming out of a shed. The fire got bigger and bigger. Someone sent for the Fire Brigade and bang, crash, there were flames 100 feet high. The people had kept gas cylinders in their shed. One of them wasn't closed properly so the gas built up until it just ignited. He had three big gas canisters in there, enough to cook a full three-course lunch. The Fire Brigade weren't very happy. (Jim Greenhill)

And there may be other reasons for sheds going up in smoke:

The chap next door had all his strawberries stolen. He reported it to the police but at that time you weren't allowed to grow soft fruit here. He was so angry he set light to his shed – the tools and everything. (Eric Sherwood)

Shed-free plots

Without a shed you have to trundle tools and other essentials in a wheelbarrow or in the back of the car.

There were no sheds so we had to take our tools with us. You always ended up with one thing you forgot to bring. (Mike and Pat Cosgrove)

Or you may be able to manage without one:

I don't have a shed – I have a hoe, fork, cultivator and rake leaning on the fence of our neighbour's plot. (Edward Probert)

In some allotments, sheds are not allowed for aesthetic reasons.

We have an exceptional location in a conservation area – a gated compound with lock and key, directly next to the Cotswold Way, with a panoramic view of Bath. Huts are not allowed, but all of us have 'trunks' and it's not an issue. (Anthony Pearson)

Outside growth

The support of a shed makes it good for growing everything from fruit such as grapes and blackberries to roses, sweet peas or any other kinds of climbers. Around the shed you can make beds for herbs and flowers.

We had hops growing over one shed. When they fruited in autumn they were great for flower arranging. On another we inherited a grapevine – one hot year we even got some fruit on it. (Ruth)

RECYCLING

Nothing's wasted on an allotment – you can use anything. I love it. Marvellous! (Sue Bryant)

People with passion for allotments are often avid recyclers, making use of anything they can. This is what helps to give allotments their character. Apart from vegetable matter suitable for composting (see p. 59) and the plastic boxes and bags to keep in the shed for harvesting, these are other good uses for recycled items.

• Milk crates – make containers for sweet peas planted in tubes. Piled in a pair with a plank on top they form a comfortable seat.

• Scratched or unwanted CDs – hang up to scare birds.

• Wood – useful for shed construction and repair, for sides of raised beds and compost heaps and sunken path edging.

• Bricks – for paths, to keep polythene and netting in place on the ground and to raise pots off the soil.

• Plastic drinks bottles – put on top of canes for safety and as bird scarers. Cut down they make watering spikes and handy devices for spraying weedkiller.

Cut off the bottom and one side of a small plastic milk carton and splay out the sides. You can then put this round a weed to isolate it – then spray. This stops spray going on to other plants. (Tim Pryce)

• Plastic food containers with holes in the base – for sowing seeds.

• Metal rods – for supporting netting.

• Strips of carpet – for suppressing weeds.

• Thick polythene wrapping from things like mattresses can be used over wire hoops or a frame to protect plants.

• Glass – to cover a home-made cold frame or small raised bed. Even better if the whole window frame is included.

• Perspex sheeting – also for cold frames and cloches.

• Old clothes – to dress a scarecrow.

• String – useful for all kinds of jobs, like tying canes for climbing beans and sweet peas.

• Bent or stained cutlery – useful tools; forks for separating seedlings, knives for weeding around plants.

• Wire coat hangers – can be cut into lengths to make fleece pegs.

• Newspapers – shredded as improvers for soil texture.

• Apple tree prunings and canes from autumn raspberries – sticks for peas.

- China.

  One of our ladies has an old machine that grinds old china to make grit to improve the soil. Everybody here keeps their eggshells and dries them out, then grinds them up. They keep off slugs and help the soil. (Sue Bryant)

- Old furniture – for the shed.

  Old cupboards make good raised beds for carrots. (Damien Grove)

- Wire mesh – for plot and bed boundaries and for peas and sweet peas.

  My husband got wire mesh from his works – they were throwing it away. (Angela Downs)

- Larger items from home renovation projects, such as tanks and sinks, which are good for collecting water and for herbs, flowers and quick-growing vegetables.

  Her water tank is an old immersion tank with pipes coming off the guttering on the side of her shed. (Sue Bryant)

WELCOME WILDLIFE

Even in the middle of London, being at the allotment is a bit like going to the country. (Ruth)

Hours spent watching buzzards and other birds, and encounters with frogs and toads are undoubtedly good for the soul, and bees and other insects are vital for getting good crops. The pristine allotment is going to be less wildlife friendly than one where at least a few areas are allowed to get seedy and overgrown – it's a matter of weighing up your priorities. Many allotment sites have boundaries that are wildlife friendly, but these may, of course, be breeding grounds for rabbits and other pests.

Bees

Bees are vital for pollinating flowers and ensuring crops of everything from courgettes and cucumbers to peas and beans. You may be lucky enough to have a bee-keeper on your site, but if not, there are ways of attracting bees to your plot. Blackberries, raspberries, loganberries and gooseberries have flowers attractive to bees, as do apple, pear and plum trees. The pretty flowers of such aromatic herbs as borage, thyme, marjoram, mint and sage are also bee magnets.

> *I discovered a good way to get lots of bees onto the plot by letting a planting of rocket bolt and flower. The bees loved it and ever since I've let an overwintered patch of rocket flower to give the bees plenty of sustenance in spring. The bonus is that you also get seed heads to collect for another sowing. (Ruth)*

If you want to grow some ornamental flowers to encourage bees even more, then good choices are lavender and dahlias. You may consider them weeds, but poppies, dead-nettles and speedwells all have bee-friendly blooms.

Wasps

The chief benefit of wasps is that the workers of the colony devour large quantities of insects, which they feed to developing grubs in return for meals of the sugary saliva the grubs produce. They only become a nuisance towards the end of the season when they seek out the sweetness of plums and other fruit. Leaving some windfall apples on the ground for wasps to feed on is a good way of helping to distract them from your picnics.

> *If I find wasps' nests I try to keep them going – they are part of the food chain. They'll clear the greenfly off the brassicas and clean them up. (Sue Bryant)*

Also welcome is the ichneumon wasp which lays its eggs in the caterpillars of cabbage whites and other caterpillars. It does not look like a wasp at all – it has an elongated body and big wings, more like a daddy-long-legs.

Hoverflies

Hoverflies look like wasps without a 'waist'. As their name suggests, they hover motionless over plants. The grubs devour huge numbers of aphids.

Ants

Ants are a mixed blessing. While they are excellent scavengers and helpful to the process of decomposition that recycles organic matter into the soil, and will also kill and eat caterpillars, many ants encourage aphids by 'farming' aphid colonies for their nectar and protecting them against ladybird predators.

> *We dug an ant's nest out of the plot and put all the soil and eggs on the allotment boundary. But the ants were back again the next year. (Ruth)*

Ladybirds

Red, yellow or orange, spotted in black, ladybirds are superb allotment scavengers. Both the adults and their larvae, known as 'garden crocodiles', are voracious devourers of the aphids and scale insects that attack allotment crops and flowers; each can eat up to 150 aphids in a single day. The eggs, mostly laid on the undersides of leaves, hatch into elongated larvae, dark grey with coloured blotches. These consume many times their own weight in other insects and their eggs before turning into the spherical pupae from which new adults hatch.

The ladybird you don't want is the harlequin. This voracious predator, the most invasive on earth, has the potential to decimate Britain's native ladybird populations. When food like greenfly and scale insects are scarce, harlequins even prey on adult ladybirds and devour butterfly eggs, caterpillars and lacewing larvae. Generally larger than British ladybirds, these American imports are usually orange with 15 to 21 black spots, or black with two or four orange or red spots. If you see one, visit www.harlequin-survey.org for more details of what to do.

Frogs and toads

Damp patches in the allotments, and the moist shelter of large leaves, are most conducive to frogs and toads, as are nearby ponds. These allotment-friendly creatures will devour insects by the hundred.

I had just put my trowel underneath a group of lovage leaves when a huge frog hopped out. I quickly stopped weeding to admire this beautiful creature, green on top and flushed orange below. It reappeared on and off in more or less the same patch of vegetation for nearly three years, then I never saw it again. (Ruth)

Frogs and toads are not to every allotment gardener's taste:

Ever since a horrid incident in the centre of Cambridge (I trod on a toad on the steps of the Department of Archaeology) I have had a dreadful fear of both toads and frogs. So, the allotment was not ideal; it had the perfect lake for breeding and rearing young toads and during the winter months they all moved onto the land to hibernate in the craggy, heavy soil. Digging in winter became a nightmare. Every time I plunged a fork into the ground I was convinced I would spike a sleeping toad. It was not made any easier by the old boys who had worked the land for years. 'Oh, yes,' they said, 'there are hundreds of toads in the soil over winter and it's impossible to avoid pronging them, I often have to remove them from my fork with my boot.' (Heather Binney)

Butterflies

Butterflies are beautiful as long as they are not cabbage whites laying eggs on your brassicas, though it is relatively easy to keep them off with netting. Like bees, butterflies are pollinators, but not as important to crop success. To attract butterflies to your allotment, plant a buddleia (which bees also love) and encourage a patch of nettles, a plant favoured by the caterpillars of peacocks, red admirals and small tortoiseshells. Meadow grasses around plot perimeters will attract meadow browns and small heaths.

We often had peacocks and small tortoiseshells hibernating in the Highgate shed. We tried hard to keep them in, to stop them flying out too early and dying of cold. (Ruth)

Hedgehogs

Hedgehogs will eat valuable worms from your plot, but will help to clear it of slugs, beetles and the like. Once resident at the allotment hedgehogs will probably find enough to eat without your assistance, but they will appreciate a place to hibernate for the winter, such as a pile of leaves or vegetation left underneath your shed.

Worms

Earthworms are invaluable to the gardener because except in the depths of winter they continually till the soil, helping to produce a fine tilth. Worms do their work by loosening, rotating and aerating the soil, and eating earth containing leaves and other organic material then excreting the remains. To encourage more worms, all you need do is keep your soil moist and regularly dig in plenty of organic matter. In a compost heap, the best worms to encourage are the red brandlings (*Eisenia foetida*). Other helpful worms are the nematodes (see p. 91), key weapons in organic pest control.

Spiders

In the autumn allotment dew-covered spiders' webs are everywhere to be seen, often attached to long strings of gossamer, spread plant to plant. Spiders are welcome on the allotment at any time of year for their ability to catch and eat insects of all kinds.

> *It looked like a big spot on a leaf but when I touched it, hundreds of tiny black and yellow spiders exploded out from it, then clustered back together again. Held together by a loose kind of web they were the next generation of allotment spiders. (Ruth)*

Birds

> *We had a raven here – you think it's a crow until you start to look at it properly. (Mike Wiffen)*

It is always a thrill when a robin pecks beside you as you are working, and as long as you keep them off your fruit and young plants, birds can do a lot of good by eating unwelcome worms and other invertebrates. Feeders will attract blue tits, finches and other small birds, but also unwelcome pigeons, so the choice is yours.

Our resident buzzard is a wonderful sight. It glides from shed to shed, sitting for as much as half an hour at a time surveying the scene. We've never seen it swoop to catch a rabbit, but it surely must have. When it flies over towards the nearby rookery, to the cedar where it nests, the other birds fly at it angrily. (Ruth)

Foxes

Allotment foxes are pests only if they actually damage your plants. In town, mangy foxes can be a distressing sight you may want to report to your local authority or RSPCA. Foxes may dig up young plants when burying surplus food, but are unlikely to eat them.

Every summer, tracks of broken stems appeared through our autumn raspberries. Only when we saw a fox strolling up towards that end of the plot in broad daylight did we put two and two together. (Ruth)

On a rabbit-infested plot foxes are welcome. They will also catch and eat rats, mice and squirrels. On the minus side, hedgehogs, frogs and birds appear on the fox's menu.

Foxes are mischievous – they dig holes. I think they are after the moles. (Sue Bryant)

Wild flowers

I have to say that this year nature has won out. (Hendrina Ellis)

All gardening is a battle against nature, but allowing some weeds to flourish in the allotment will encourage visits from butterflies and other insects and provide dark, damp areas for animals like frogs. You can also use a good crop of nettles to make your own organic fertilizer (see p. 59) and nettle and dandelion leaves, picked young, are excellent salad ingredients. Even if you don't like weeds on your own plot, the allotment perimeter can be a diverse habitat for wild plants.

> *At the plot, on spring and summer mornings, I always keep an eye on the scarlet pimpernels. If the flowers close up before two in the afternoon (their daily closing time) then it is almost sure to rain. (Ruth)*

And you may even find something surprising:

> *I've got wild raspberries in the allotment – I had a bit that was overgrown. I cleared out a blackcurrant among the couch grass. I hit the weeds with weedkiller and put a 3-inch mulch on it then I saw these shoots and they were wild raspberries. I've let them grow and they're a beautiful flavour. (Chris Luck)*

Rarer sightings

It is a real thrill to find rarer wildlife on your plot, whether hummingbird hawk moths – visitors to southern Britain in warm summers – rare caterpillars, adders or newts. If you should see an adder, our only poisonous snake, which may be sunbathing on your plot to warm up in springtime, leave it to its own devices.

> *We had a snake up here once – a grass snake. (Eric Sherwood)*

If you encourage the rarer species, there are also bonuses for pest control:

> *I've always had an old log pile. I've had lizards nesting under there – I moved a piece and there was also a baby slow-worm. With those I've never had to worry about slugs at all. We get pygmy shrews as well. (Maureen Nightingale)*

ALLOTMENT TREASURE

Allotment produce is wonderful but it's exciting to dig up more solid treasure from the plot. The 'hard' wealth of your allotment – whether fossils, coins or pottery shards – will depend on the history of the landscape, but there can be few plots as productive as this one at Stony Stratford.

Because we're an old established site and the Romans came through, I've found all kinds of things. I'm always finding stems and stalks of old pipes. You find all kinds of bits and pieces. Some of the other things I've collected are:

– An Italian silver fork, glass bottle fragments, Taylor's mustard pots;
– Clay and glass marbles that come from bottle tops;
– Old cheap crockery that people used to win at the fair which was held
    next door – they threw it over the hedge;
– Second World War uniform buttons;
– A French metal belt buckle;
– Flints and animals' bones and teeth;
– Fossils from the river that flooded this land;
– Crockery and pieces of iron that the old boys would throw in and which
    in its way fertilizes the ground;
– An iron S-shaped hook (my prize) – with a swan's head. It's only an inch
    and a half long. (Sue Bryant)

In Dorchester there is a different story, where the most productive allotments are land once used as dumps.

Years ago – going back 90 years – it was a rubbish dump, including the hospital. It was then backfilled with soil. We've had the bottle diggers here and I've dug up a few valuable ones. I've found a 1911 Coronation teapot and some fossilized wood 150 million years old. (Doug Chainey)

GIVING UP YOUR ALLOTMENT

However passionate you may be, keeping an allotment going doesn't always work out. Circumstances change, illness may strike, and for all sorts of reasons people find that they can't cope with their plots.

I only gave it up because I was travelling so much. You can't expect other people to weed and hoe. (Pat Bence)

Or you may, unfortunately, find your allotment threatened or actually taken over.

Where our plot was is now the M27. (Mike Cosgrove)

The takeover of land for building can thwart the most ambitious of allotment plans:

A friend of mine has a little vineyard and when he pruned one year he gave me cuttings and nearly every one struck. My intention was to enter a bottle of wine from them in the Summer Show from my own grapes. I planted four rows, wired and trained them up and had one crop. Then the builders came and I lost the lot. (Robin Barrett)

CHAPTER 2

ON THE PLOT

BEGINNINGS

It's all trial and error. (Mike Cosgrove)

So you have your plot. Unless it is brand new and the ground has been prepared for you in advance it probably won't have been cultivated for some time, so the first thing you'll need to do is to clear it. For that you'll need a spade and fork – as well as muscle power and persistence. And even if it has been rotovated you certainly won't be immune from weeds.

On large sites, allotments are usually allocated to newcomers in autumn or winter so that new tenants have the time to clear and dig the site before weeds burgeon again in the spring. Even so, it may take months – or years – of dogged cultivation to get the plot into the shape you want.

> *Our first allotment was more than waist high with grass. It looked a daunting task. The first thing we did was shear the vegetation to a reasonable height. We then dug the strip in the middle, taking out as many roots as we could possibly find, and planted some radishes and lettuces, while we started on the plot ends. (Ruth)*

As you begin to clear the weeds you may make some unexpected finds:

When I took this plot over it was up to here [thigh height] in grass and I discovered a whole lot of strawberries. They were lovely. The grass was making a greenhouse for them. (Eric Sherwood)

Spit by spit

The only successful way of clearing a plot, although painstaking and time-consuming is probably to dig it spit by spit – and to double depth if there are loads of roots of convolvulus and the like – pulling up weeds and removing their roots as you go and chucking out stones. If you know it's going to take more than one summer and autumn, covering the areas you're not going to be able to dig with carpet or thick black polythene (weighted down) will help to suppress any additional growth of weeds.

We had to start from scratch on a plot 'turfed' with field grass. It was on land we were given to use on the edge of playing fields. We dug it by hand. It was really hard work getting it organized. (Mike Cosgrove)

The first year was murder – just to dig a row was 15 minutes. Now you can do it in a minute. (Ken Daniels)

If you're tempted to rotovate, think twice. While you'll be saving on muscle you may just be cutting the roots of perennial weeds into little pieces and spreading them around.

Someone rotovated my allotment and spread ground elder everywhere. (Sue Bryant)

Another alternative is to treat very weedy areas with a weedkiller like gyphosate before you dig. This is best done in late summer, when plants are still growing actively. Even though the manufacturers say that you can cultivate six weeks after treatment, you will need to leave double this time to be on the safe side, and it is an expensive way to treat a big area.

As you dig you can begin incorporating manure, but don't think this is the end of the weeds – it's likely to take you several seasons and more to get them under control. Planting potatoes is a good way to help clear a plot and they will certainly help suppress annual weeds. Because potatoes are regularly earthed up during their growing season, many weeds are prevented from getting a hold. Luxuriant potato foliage will also shade weeds and limit their growth. Other vegetables that exert this shading effect to some extent include squashes, marrows and pumpkins.

Planning the plot

By all means put quick-maturing crops into the plot straight away, but take time to plan out what you want to grow, and where you want to put permanent crops like raspberries, asparagus, artichokes and perennial herbs. You also need to think where you want paths – possibly up the centre and across the middle of the plot as well as around the edges, but these may form themselves as you begin working and walking around the plot. Even if you do not make raised beds, there is a virtue in planning things so that you do not have to tread on the soil too much:

> *I dug three plots then divided them into two so I have six areas and can reach into the centre of them all to save walking on them. (Marta Scott)*

Other areas may also evolve as you work the plot, but you may also want to make space for a greenhouse, a shed, a picnic and barbecue area, a mini lawn for relaxing, a herb and/or flower garden …. But there is no need to do it all at once.

> *Having a new allotment is a bit like moving into a new house. You need to live with it for a while before you see how best to organize it. (Ruth)*

The ends of the plot are good places for permanent plantings and can serve the dual purpose of adding some privacy and acting as a windbreak. Also tall plants like artichokes will make a lot of shade, so ends and sides are good for these. An asparagus bed works well across the middle of the plot, but can also go at one end.

> *When we took on the Dorset plot we decided that **this time** we were going to be more organized from the beginning. So we designated and cleared a patch at one end for the autumn raspberries, between an existing gooseberry and some healthy*

rhubarb. Also, when we had the rabbit-proof fencing put up we had extra wires added along one side for training a cultivated blackberry. We are still battling the convolvulus, though. (Ruth)

Otherwise, you will need to plan to plant crops and rotate them so that, ideally, you only grow the same thing in the same position every three years. This is especially necessary to help reduce the risk of diseases like club root.

Proper crop rotation can be tricky if some parts of your plot have better soil, are less windy and so on, but if you plan to have produce all year round, crop rotation will largely take care of itself. Overwintering brassicas like purple sprouting broccoli will still be in the ground by the time you are sowing seeds of crops like peas, beetroot and parsnips in spring.

Certain vegetables help each other, so you put broad beans next to potatoes, onions next to beetroot and leeks next to tomatoes. Runner beans, onions and tomatoes can stay in the same place for up to three years. (David Downton)

The other thing you'll need to consider if you're using farmyard manure is that you won't be able to grow root vegetables in it until it has been well rotted down, which may take a year or more.

TOOLS

I always look in the market for tools. If you see anything blacksmith-made – grab it. (Mike Wiffen)

Once you have the basics you can add to your tool collection as you go along. If you share the work with someone else, it helps to have your own individual spades, forks and trowels. Try all tools in the hand before you buy; a tool needs to feel comfortable while you are working and weeding the soil. Good stainless steel tools are an excellent investment.

Also useful are multi-purpose tools, many of which you can take on and off handles of different lengths.

I've got a reversible tool which is a three-pronged hoe on one side and a two-edged-cut hoe on the other. With one side you can stir up the soil and with the other you can cut off the weeds. I have a big one and a little one. (Chris Luck)

If your shed is dry you should not have too much problem with rust, but good tools are worth keeping clean and, occasionally, oiled. On a wet, muddy day, try to make time to scrape off as much surplus soil as possible from your tools before you leave.

Starting on all this digging and cutting back has made me clean and sharpen all the tools. I've taken them all to bits and cleaned them up. (Ann Tucker)

Spades, forks and shovels

These are needed for or digging. Young people, and some women, prefer small ladies' versions. A shovel can be useful (and efficient) for moving piles of compost or soil.

On London clay I rarely used a spade, the ground was too heavy, but on light chalk a fork just doesn't do the job. (Ruth)

I've got a fork I'd never be without – it's stainless steel. (Sue Bryant)

Trowels and hand forks

You need these for weeding, sowing and all kinds of small-scale tasks. While some people like a wide-bladed trowel others favour the narrower sort. A hand fork is good for weeding, especially prising out the roots of invasive perennials.

For weeding you can also improvise:

Get an old kitchen knife and bend it at a right angle. You can then use it to get around plants. (Tim Pryce)

Hoes

Essential for weeding, these come in many designs and you may want to experiment to see which suit you best. A Dutch hoe, with a flat, thin blade is the classic weeding hoe; a draw hoe has a blade at right angles to the handle. There is also a short-handled version, traditionally called an onion hoe, good for working close to plants.

> *My favourite instrument is a hoe to chop them [weeds] off. If you're using an old hoe you need a stone to keep it sharp. You keep hitting stones so it blunts up. (Mike Wiffen)*

> *I've got a small hand hoe and the 'forky' version which work well for me. (Sue Bryant)*

Rake

A single rake should be all you need for levelling the soil, ideally light and easy to use.

Secateurs

Secateurs are necessary for dealing with fruit, but also for all kinds of other cutting jobs; the sort in which only one of the blades moves is now more common than the scissor-style.

Shears

Shears are needed for grass edges if you have no strimmer, and are useless unless kept properly sharp.

> *How many times have we tried to cut allotment edges with blunt shears at the beginning of the year? Now we have a strimmer, but before that we never seemed to be ahead of the game. (Ruth)*

Wheelbarrow

A wheelbarrow is handy on the plot, but not essential if you have a small shed (or none) and nowhere to keep one at home. It's also useful for carrying things to and from home if you live close by. You may easily be able to borrow one from a neighbour.

Power tools

These are useful for the allotment only if petrol driven or cordless. Big ones, like rotovators, are best borrowed or hired, but a strimmer is useful for edges and rough areas.

WHAT WILL YOU GROW?

You have to try everything. (Sue Bryant)

The answer is, whatever you and your family like to eat – and what you're able to store, freeze or preserve over the winter – as well as experimenting with new varieties and more unusual crops to see how they do and whether you like them. If they're not a success then you don't have to grow them another year.

I like growing unusual things – things the supermarkets don't do very well. I've been quite successful with pak choi, globe artichokes and fennel. (Vicky Scott)

And there is no shame in sticking to what you know.

We're not adventurous – we keep to the same old basics. When we do branch out we usually find it's a failure. (Anthony Pearson)

The thrill of having your first allotment is well amplified by some quick, easy vegetables.

The first things I grew were radishes, then beetroot and French beans. I put them in really late but they soon caught up. (Marta Scott)

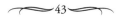

The soil on your plot – and the protection you're able to provide for the more tender plants – will also have a bearing on what you grow.

> *I have a shed at home but I grow more 'pick to eat' because I don't have much storage space. (Vicky Scott)*

If you love fresh vegetables, try planning for every season so that you always have something to pick, even just a few rocket leaves for a winter salad.

> *We like to grow fairly small quantities of lots of different things, but there are always gluts. It's so difficult to avoid the temptation of saving every seedling. (Ruth)*

WIND AND WEATHER

You can guarantee that on an allotment no two years will ever be the same, though you will quickly become aware of the general run of the weather from year to year. Nevertheless, there seems no obvious reason why crops like parsnips and broad beans do brilliantly one year and fail completely the next.

> *It's always terribly, terribly variable. (Anthony Pearson)*

> *What comes up comes up – what doesn't, doesn't. (Damien Grove)*

Of course plot holders – like farmers and other gardeners – always moan about the weather, about the prevalence of pests and diseases and such. Some fruit and vegetables do respond quite predictably to the weather.

> *A hot summer, with lots of watering needed, meant that Brussels sprouts, sprouting broccoli and celeriac were slow to grow and the fennel hardly got going. But the courgettes, cucumbers and chillis loved it. And we ate raspberries every day from July to October.*

A wet, cold summer, with high winds, blew the flowers off the runner beans and the bean sticks were in danger of collapsing completely. The cucumbers were slow to fruit and the onions got mildew. Tomatoes and potatoes were hit by blight. But the purple sprouting broccoli was magnificent, so too were the Brussels sprouts once they were staked. The beetroots were huge and juicy. (Ruth)

Many allotment vegetables are not frost hardy, but with the help of cloches and cold frames, fleece and other protection – and a greenhouse if you're lucky – there is a lot you can do to cheat the seasons. Equally, if you improve your soil so as to maximize fertility, water retention and drainage, you are also sure to enhance the health and prospects of your plants.

THE ANNUAL ROUND

Out in the allotment you can almost tell what month it is by the smell of the air and the feel of the soil. (Ruth)

The allotment year takes on a regular rhythm – seed sowing in spring and early summer, digging and composting in autumn and winter. Late summer brings the height of the harvest and also the time to sow seeds of autumn vegetables like pak choi and last crops of rocket and other quick-maturing crops like the newest varieties of dwarf beans.

It is always a sad moment when the runner bean sticks have to be taken down. I always wonder if I'll be here next year to put them up again. (Don Binney)

Because it is impossible to rely on the weather being consistent from year to year, it makes sense to time your tasks by the season and not the calendar.

CLOTHES

When working the plot you need to be comfortable, warm and dry and protected as far as possible from abrasions on your knees and legs, arms and hands. Since it is impossible to garden properly without getting dirty, a collection of old clothes is essential. Or you may like to wear dungarees or an all-in-one worker's overall.

Wellingtons are good for winter and wet weather, or you may prefer stout boots. For the summer, trainers or sturdy light shoes are generally more practical than sandals.

One of the joys of gardening is feeling the soil and plants in your hands, but this is not everyone's experience. Gloves are handy in the winter when digging, and essential for jobs like pruning gooseberries, but are a hindrance when transplanting. Some gardeners keep boxes of disposable plastic gloves in their sheds. These are fine if you can stand the feel of them. Many of the cheaper sorts of gloves wear out very quickly, and even the more expensive ones are vulnerable.

It must be the way I weed. However much I pay for a pair, invariably the thumb on the left-hand glove wears out long before any other part of the glove. (Ruth)

DIGGING AND ROTOVATING

On a crisp, late autumn day there are few jobs more satisfying than digging the allotment. There are conflicting views about the merits of digging, and how deep you should go. You also need to consider the soil, since very light soils can be damaged, and their water retention destroyed by too much disturbance. It is always unwise to dig when the soil is very wet and soggy, and you should never touch it when it is cold and frozen.

Digging turns and churns the soil and is an excellent means of helping to get rid of stones and perennial weeds, which you need to pick out meticulously as you dig every spadeful, getting every little piece of root if you can. This is not always as easy as it sounds:

You dig down a short way and you hit rock. One is forever digging up stones the size of a fist. One person on the plot next to mine levered out a boulder about 18 inches across. (Anthony Pearson)

When I dig I feel as if I'm mining, there are so many stones. And the couch grass is thick, too. (Marta Scott)

It is a good idea to throw perennial and annual weeds into separate buckets or big plastic 'baskets' as you work (if your ground is stony keep an extra one beside you for those). As you dig, add manure or compost. Once the ground has been cleared you can simply put a thick top dressing of manure onto it in autumn, leave the worms to do their work over the winter, then fork in the remainder in spring. This is especially good for light, chalky or sandy soils.

On heavy, London clay we dug every autumn. In Dorset, where the soil is light and chalky, light forking or very shallow digging is all that's needed apart from tackling any deep-rooted weeds. I've discovered it's true, as they say around here, that you should never do any serious digging between April and September. (Ruth)

Dig with a spade or a fork, depending on your strength and the type of soil you have. On a large piece of ground it pays to be systematic, and to have any compost or manure that you're going to add in a wheelbarrow or heap nearby. When you dig the first trench, take the soil from this to the far end of the area you are working on to fill in the final one. Put compost or manure into this first trench, then cover it with the soil from the next trench, and so on. To double dig you literally double the process, going two spits or spade depths down with each trench.

Everyone develops their own digging technique, but to spare strain on your back there are a few good tips.

• Keep the spade or fork at right angles to the soil, your back straight and your knees bent as you push into the ground.

• Don't try to move too much earth at once.

• When you need to remove weeds or stones, or add compost, be sure to bend your knees.

• Dig little and often.

If you can isolate annual weeds, or have leafy remains to get rid of, put them straight into the bottom of your trenches.

Rotovating – and more

If you find digging too hard, a petrol-driven rotovator, either borrowed or hired, may be the answer to your problems, but you may need to get someone to do the job for you and you need to be wary of how you plant.

If you have a small rotovator plant your crops in rows slightly farther apart than the tines – this will enable you to run it up and down the rows and keep the weeds down. (Tim Callard)

But beware if you have perennial weed problems. The rotovator will cut the roots up into tiny pieces and spread them around. Not what you want.

On extremely big country plots it's not unknown for proper ploughing to be done.

When I first took this plot over they were much bigger. One chap had three, and actually brought a plough in and ploughed them. He asked me if I'd like mine done – at a price. (Eric Sherwood)

SOIL

I try to make the soil do whatever I want it to do. (Vicky Scott)

To grow good produce you do need a good layer of topsoil into which plant roots can penetrate to absorb water and nutrients. When you've cleared a new plot of weeds you may be a bit disappointed.

I've found the soil is heavy and there is not much topsoil. I've been using garden centre organic compost to improve it. (Marta Scott)

The soil you'll get at your allotment will depend on where you live, although probably a mixture will tend towards one of the four basic types – clay, chalk, sand and peat. Just looking around an allotment site will give you a good idea of what grows well, and it's worth asking the old hands about the allotment soil before you take on your plot.

Listen to people in the know. (Damien Grove)

There will doubtless be moans, groans and shaking of heads by those who grow the biggest and best vegetables and fruit, but at least they'll tell you what kind of soil you're taking on.

The truth is that, as my father always said, 'What you get out of the soil depends on what you put into it.' (Ruth)

You can do much to improve what you inherit, but you'll still have to tend your plot according to what you get.

The soil is quite light – there are a lot of flints. If you dig two feet down you hit a compacted layer of big stones with extremely well-established bindweed that's been there for centuries. (Edward Probert)

All soils need extra organic matter added on a regular basis to improve and maintain them. Even after many years you may never achieve the ideal of porous, open but nutrient rich loam that is the textbook ideal (technically a mixture of 20–25% clay, 30–35% chalk and 40–50% sand), but it is worth persisting.

The nearest thing I've ever seen to loam was the soil on my father's allotment, where the naturally fertile 'Devon red' was enhanced with compost upon compost. The giant cauliflowers, potatoes and other vegetables he grew were, he said, the happy outcome of 'lots in, lots out'. (Ruth)

We have a loam-based soil with gravel underneath so it's quite fertile once it gets going. (Ann Tucker)

Feeling the soil will give you an idea of its type and structure. If you wet your hands, then pick up a handful of soil and roll it around, clay will quickly form itself into a sausage shape while chalk or sand will quickly break up.

A very weedy, uncultivated allotment also contains clues about the soil you're getting. Lots of creeping buttercups are a sign of waterlogged acid soil, while scarlet pimpernels and thistles flourish on chalk. Dandelions will grow almost anywhere but are likely to be profuse on heavy soils. On the plus side, nettles are a sign that the soil is fertile and rich in nitrogen, as are fat hen, chickweed, couch grass and thistles.

Clay

Made up of fine particles, clay soil can be brown, grey or yellow. It retains water very well (in fact too well), which makes it slow to drain. When dry it forms a hard, thick, cement-like crust, making it almost impossible to work. It is also slow to heat up in spring, so is poor for plants needing a good start. The great advantage of clay is that it is essentially very fertile, but because it is usually acid it will benefit from the addition of lime, particularly if you want to grow good brassicas, though you need to do this at least a month before you put in plants or seeds. Also, you must keep liming well separated from manuring (because the two react together to make ammonia). Mushroom compost, being alkaline, is great for clay soils.

Good, regular treatment will improve clay well and leave you with a soil that has the advantage of keeping moist even in dry spells.

We have a lot of Essex clay – I like it because I get it dug over really well then manure it and leave it for the worms to take down. (Maureen Nightingale)

Any kind of grit will help break up clay and make it drain better, but best is probably pea shingle or horticultural gravel or coarse sand (though not the builder's variety).

Shredded and dug in, piles and piles of newspaper were an economy addition to the London clay of our Highgate plot. Put in the bottom of trenches as we worked in autumn (with many pauses to read past headlines and cricket scores) it was already well rotted in by the following spring and improved the soil really well. After finding lots of sheets nibbled by rodents, however, we kept our shed supplies of newsprint on high shelves and in plastic bags to discourage them. (Ruth)

Chalk

Chalky soil is virtually the opposite of clay and can look pure white when dry. It is flimsy and drains so quickly that even after a whole day's rain the soil can be bone dry within 24 hours. Chalk's alkalinity can impair plant health, making growth poor and, when extreme, turning leaves yellow in a condition called chlorosis. Well-rotted leaf mould, horse manure and garden compost will all help to bump up the soil acidity as well as improving water retention. No lime is needed. Growing green manures is another good way of improving chalky soils and mulching helps too.

> On light Dorset chalk which drains and dries so quickly, annual loads of rotted horse manure have helped massively, but in dry spells there is endless carrying of watering cans. Mulches of bark put round strawberries immediately after rain have helped, but it is a constant battle. (Ruth)

> If you use grass clippings only apply them 2 inches deep as they can produce too much heat. (Tim Callard)

> We had an allotment in Cambridge adjacent to a disused quarry which was filled with water and had plenty of wildlife. Our soil was rich in chalk and clay and consequently set rock-hard in the summer so it was a miracle any plants managed to break through the surface at all. In the winter months it became a heavy mess, reminiscent of the Somme and extremely difficult to dig. (Heather Binney)

Sand

The great advantages of sandy soil, which slips easily through the fingers, is that it drains well and warms up quickly in spring, making it ideal for early crops. Like chalky ones, sandy soils need plenty of organic material added on a regular basis to give them more bulk and to improve their ability to retain water.

> With sand the water whips straight through – you lose every bit of water you ever had. (Chris Luck)

We have very sandy soil which requires lots of manure; fortunately, I have been able to get plenty of good rotted horse manure. This year [2007] we have not had to water! (Andrew Malleson)

Green manures and mulches are also ideal for sandy soils.

Peat

Dark and rich, peat soils are naturally rich in humus but often have a poor structure which leads to inadequate drainage. Rather than adding loads of compost, you need coarse sand or pea shingle, as with clay soils, for improving peat. If the soil is very acidic you will also need to add lime or chalk every year or two.

Acid or alkaline?

For allotment fruit and vegetables the ideal soil, especially if you want to grow brassicas or root crops like turnips, is one that is slightly alkaline. Although you can get a good idea of what your soil is like from what your neighbours are growing and doing, the scientific way of measuring is with a soil-testing kit. A reading of anything above 7 is alkaline, below 7 acid.

BOUNDARIES AND PATHS

When you take on your plot it should be obvious where it begins and ends. The chances are that there will be at least one edge of your plot with a grass surround. A solid path, if there is one, may be gravel or tarmac and in any kind of repair.

It is amazing how quickly grass and other weeds from the allotment boundary can encroach onto your plot, especially in late spring. To keep grass at bay, it helps to have some kind of barrier. Wood works fine, but will rot in a few years and will need to be regularly renewed. Bricks are excellent, but expensive unless you have access to a load of unwanted ones. Cheaper is flexible plastic border edging, though you need the sort that is 15 cm (6 in) wide, at least. A buried fences of the kind you need to keep out rabbits is also effective.

Endless edging. With a plot surrounded on three sides by grass, in the days before the invention of the invaluable cordless strimmer, we seemed to be constantly edging. Neat vertical cuts with a spade, and the addition of a load of lengths of wood (mostly from skips) helped a lot, but hours were spent with shears. We managed somehow, but our boundaries were never really very neat and tidy. (Ruth)

If you are lucky, your council or neighbours may mow the grass between plots, but even this is unlikely to get right up to the edges. Only persistent cutting and weeding will keep your edges tidy, but don't get too obsessed.

As a beginner, I was advised to get some things in and not worry about the paths, so that's what I did. (Marta Scott)

If you use a strimmer to keep your boundaries neat, a petrol one is the best choice. The average 'charge life' of the battery kind is only about 30 minutes which means that you probably have to allow more than one session to get all the way round.

I inherited a shed along with an antique push mower. I have used it, but now I have a petrol strimmer instead. (Robin Barrett)

With a hard path you may be able to scrape weeds off with a spade, or even isolate them enough to kill them off with a weedkiller such as glyphosate. Some, like wild blackberries – or cultivated ones that have been propagated with the help of birds – may even be useful and trainable.

If your neighbours have plants at the edge of their plots that encroach onto yours (or yours to theirs) then you may need to be diplomatic and generous when it comes to cutting back and harvesting. Such issues are usually easily resolved and far less contentious than weed problems.

We shared a blackberry 'hedge' with our neighbour. Luckily they weren't his favourite fruit so we enjoyed them all and in return did the cutting back on both sides. (Ruth)

Paths

Depending on how you like to organize your planting, and whether you favour growing plants in rows right across the plot, you may want to make a path up the middle of the allotment, and possibly across it as well. If well and frequently trodden, paths like this will keep relatively clear of grass and other weeds, but you may want to invest in wooden planks or even stone slabs to cut down on work.

> *We had new paths laid at home and took all the old slabs down to the allotment to make a central path. The effect is excellent – so much tidier. (Ruth)*

Strips of old carpet, which are excellent for suppressing weeds, do get very soggy in winter. Nor do they last for ever and can be a trip hazard if they get holes in them. As with allotment borders, edging of some kind along paths helps orderliness and discourages weeds.

> *On our allotments one chap has put down thick plastic and covered it with bark to make paths between his beds. It looks OK but I'm just letting mine go to grass. (John Makin)*

TREES AND OVERHANGS

Trees on an allotment can be a blessing if they are good fruit trees but a curse if they create too much shade, sap valuable water from the soil or deposit tons of unwanted leaves on your allotment every autumn. And trees are 'home' to unwanted allotment wildlife like squirrels and pigeons.

A tree that's actually growing on your plot is most likely to be a fruit tree of some kind. If it is healthy and productive then it is worth keeping, but otherwise you may want to cut it down. This may or may not be allowed – you will need to check with your allotment committee or the local council, and for health and safety reasons you are likely to need the services of a professional. When planning the removal, find out about having the roots extracted, for they will still provide an inhospitable barrier to most vegetables.

*I've got a lot of shade but it's private. We took all the growth off – we got the
ladder out and chopped it off. (Reg Simmons)*

Underneath existing trees, shallow-rooted raspberries can be persuaded to thrive if they
are given a generous top dressing of manure, or you may like to plant daffodils and
other spring bulbs. As long as you can keep it confined, mint will do well under a tree.
Or you may just like to sow some grass seed around the base and, when it's well grown,
have a wooden seat there to relax on.

Trees growing outside the allotment boundary are a different matter altogether.
These are the responsibility of the people on whose land they are growing, who may be
homeowners or, if the trees are in the road, the local council. Although, in law, you are
entitled to cut back any parts of trees that overhang your 'property' this can be unwise –
if not physically impossible with the equipment you have to hand. Rather than marching
round to the neighbour's house and demanding action, try getting the problem dealt
with by your allotment committee. You may or may not be lucky.

In autumn, leaves of deciduous trees that fall on your plot are best scooped up and
composted in a separate bin, if you have the space, or bagged up for recycling. Pine
needles are only fit for the bonfire.

Old, tall trees can be an allotment hazard if they are likely to shed large branches,
or even come down completely in a high wind. A plot near trees like this is not one on
which it is wise to risk having a greenhouse.

If you decide to plant a tree on your plot, think about what it should be, the
problems it may bring with it, and how big it will grow. Also, if it is an apple, pear or
plum tree, and depending on the fruit growing in your neighbours' plots, think about
whether you need two trees to ensure proper fertilization. If you have any doubts about
whether trees are allowed, check with your allotment committee or, failing that, with the
council or whoever owns the plot.

*If flower arranging is your passion, ornamental trees like eucalyptus on the
allotment boundary can be good value. We inherited one of these but not, to our
daughter's disappointment, a koala to go with it! (Ruth)*

RAISED BEDS

Many allotment gardeners swear by raised beds. Their great advantages are that they can help to combat the problem of perennial weeds and, if made to the right proportions, mean that you never have to tread on the soil in order to work the ground – and they don't need to be dug. Depending on the size and shape of your allotment they can be squares or rectangles; the latter have the advantage of being least wasteful of space. You can cover a raised bed with polythene or fleece to make a 'mega cloche' and, if you wish, provide the special conditions needed by fussy plants like blueberries, which will only grow on acid soil.

When you begin marking out your raised beds with pegs and string, remember not to forget about the paths in between.

You need to be sure you make the paths between your beds wide enough for a wheelbarrow – at least. (John Makin)

Ideally, beds should be 1.2 to 2 m (4–6 ft) wide, depending on how long your arms are, making as good use as possible of the space you have. For the sides you can use timber boards of any kind, or interlocking plastic sections now available, but best of all, say some are …

… so-called gravel boards – long treated planks about 18 ft long and 8 in deep. I set them out so that on hands and knees I can reach the middle of the beds from both sides, which means that I never have to walk on the sticky, claggy clay on a bed of limestone, which is very fertile. Raised beds have revolutionized things for me. (John Makin)

You need to dig shallow channels to sink the sides in, and fix them at the corners and at about 1-m (3-ft) intervals along the sides to pressure-treated fencing posts. Two or three board depths will give you the height you need. As you work, check to make sure everything is square and level.

Wood gleaned from skips and other kinds of driftwood can also be put to good use:

When I walk the dogs along the River Crouch I end up with wood and driftwood from the wharf (where they unload timber from Russia and planks take a dive) stuck under each arm for the allotment's raised beds and paths. (Ron Pankhurst)

If perennial weeds menace your plot, you may want to line the base of the beds with thick weed-proof fabric. A base lining of pea gravel will also help drainage. You can then fill the bed with compost and/or topsoil. Whatever you choose it does need to be as weed free as possible, so choose your topsoil carefully.

I'm using my own compost and waiting for it to build up rather than moving or buying topsoil for my new beds. (John Makin)

Raised beds are also a boon for the less able-bodied:

As you get older raised beds are an advantage. (Richard Harding)

To be effective for those with back problems and other disabilities raised beds need to be about 75 cm (30 in) high and no wider than 1.5 m (60 in) so that the soil within can be reached easily for preparation, planting and weeding.

COMPOST AND MANURE

I compost everything. (Sue Bryant)

Making good compost is one of the most satisfying allotment jobs. It is easy enough just to pile up compostable green stuff in an allotment corner, but this will quickly become unsightly and unmanageable – though hopefully not as tall as the huge mound we inherited with the Highgate plot.

For the first year and a half we left the 'horrible heap' as it was, growing a healthy crop of grass and other weeds. When we eventually delved into it we

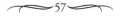

discovered superb rotted material, though mixed with lots of stones. Having decided that the best idea was to dig it out, we took turns at riddling it into a wheelbarrow. The result was a magnificent top dressing that we used on about half the plot. The ground where the heap had been was also wonderfully fertile, having been both fed and left fallow. (Ruth)

The first requisite for neat composting is a container or containers. On a large plot the ideal is a double bin, with each section about a metre square, so that the contents of one can be rotting down while the other one is filling up. The classic design is of slatted wood – another great use for old timber, skip finds and the like. Ideally the slats on the front of each section need to be slotted so that they can easily be removed. Failing perfection, solid pieces of board will make serviceable bin fronts.

I take all my rubbish over and put it in the compost bin – I should have a double, but it's all about the room. (Doug Chainey)

I made some bins out of old pallets, and as long as you turn them every couple of months they're fine. (John Makin)

A quicker way to make a serviceable composter is with reinforced chicken wire, though it needs to be pretty solid to prevent the weight of compost collapsing the sides. If you only have space for a single bin, you may well be able to get one at cut price from your local council. These are usually plastic with some kind of opening in the base, although the contents are not always easy to extract. It is best to empty these out completely every year or so, remove what's useable, and return the rest to the bin with the least rotted stuff at the bottom.

To keep composting going the heap or bin needs to be moist – but not soaking wet – well aerated and, above all, warm. It's always worth watering the compost heap in dry weather, or adding some damp grass cuttings on top to keep it moist.

If you're starting from scratch, put a layer of well-rotted compost into the bottom of the bin to get it going (it will also contain helpful worms that eat, mix and digest organic matter). On top of this, the ideal is alternate layers of wet waste (such as vegetable leaves and kitchen peelings) and drier material, ideally chopped up a bit. If you can layer in grass cuttings with this dry stuff this helps prevent slime.

If you need additional activation, add a commercial compost enhancer like Garotter or, if you're able to gather enough, nettle manure. This is made by half filling a bucket with chopped nettles, topping it up with water and leaving it for three or four weeks to 'mature'. The drained solution (take a big kitchen colander up to the allotment for the process) can then be watered onto the heap.

Covering a heap with polythene – weighed down with bricks or big stones to prevent it from being blown away – will help keep the heat in and stop it being flooded. A heap or bin that is too wet is slimy and reeks of ammonia. It may also have clouds of insects hovering above it. Turning is the best remedy at any time of year, but ace composters will turn their heaps every autumn and spring.

If you have space and patience, you can keep one bin or heap exclusively for rotting down leaves into leaf mould. It will take at least two years to get good compost, but it is excellent stuff. You can now buy biodegradable sacks for leaves which make them much more manageable.

I bring down all the leaves I can find from the garden to make leaf mould.
(Maureen Nightingale)

What to put on the compost heap
From the plot:
- Any healthy leafy material – dead leaves and soft vegetable trimmings, including rhubarb leaves;
- Annual weeds;
- Pods from shelled broad beans and peas.

But not …
- Perennial weeds;
- Very woody stems and roots – like old Brussels sprouts;
- Diseased plants like blighted tomatoes (these are best burned if bonfires are allowed);
- Potatoes – they are sure to sprout.

From home:
You will need to be well organized to bag up kitchen and home garden material for the allotment compost heap but all the following are worth including.

Include ...
• Vegetable peelings;
• Eggshells;
• Grass cuttings (within reason);
• Coffee grounds, tea bags and tea leaves;
• Shredded woody material;
• Shredded paper and thin cardboard.

But avoid ...
• Fallen leaves (unless you can compost them separately and give them a long time to rot down;
• Meat and bones – magnets for vermin;
• Animal litter and faeces;
• Glossy paper.

Growing success

There are compost heap bonuses – both accidental and deliberate. You can plant potatoes directly into the heap, which works very well for an early crop of new potatoes.

We once had a great crop of new potatoes from an old heap onto which we had thrown rejects from a main crop the previous autumn. After that we deliberately planted some first earlies, which did really well. (Ruth)

You can use heaps or bins of compost for courgettes and the like, to the benefit of crops and heap.

I get a big flower pot and cut the bottom out and push it hard into the compost heap. I put compost in it and plant courgettes. The compost heap rots down that

*much quicker because of the watering. It makes the heap look better too.
(Maureen Nightingale)*

Buying it in

Do-it-yourself composting is all very well but most people are unlikely to be able to make enough compost to feed a 10-rod plot – or even one half this size. Alternatives are most restricted in the city where, unless you live near a city farm, it may be impossible to get hold of rotted animal manure. The best solutions are mushroom compost (which your society may be able to order for you), dried poultry manure (pellets) or concentrated manure sold under proprietary names such as 'Super Dug'. None of these is perfect. Mushroom compost is expensive and not great for chalky or alkaline soils, while concentrated manure, while it goes a long way, does little to improve the water-retaining properties of light soil.

> *Bags of mushroom compost put on our asparagus every year on London clay fed it very well. (Ruth)*

Country allotmenters have more choices, and you are likely to have farmers, stables and smallholders willing to sell you well-rotted animal manure (usually horse or chicken) by the bagful or trailer load or half load.

> *Horse manure is good, but it has to be on straw or it won't rot down. (John Makin)*

If you're lucky you will be able to have manure or compost delivered right to the actual plot, but you may have to put up with having it dumped at the site entrance, and move it yourself by the barrow load. If you can't cope with shifting this yourself, hiring teenage muscle power is a good alternative.

If the gates or entrance to your allotment are kept locked, you may need to be available to receive a delivery of compost or manure, or get an allotment neighbour to do so for you.

> *Our supplier, the wonderfully named Jim the Manure Mogul, makes his winter deliveries at eight o'clock at night, making warm clothes and torch essential for our 'assignation'. (Ruth)*

Chicken pellets

Composted chicken manure pressed into compact pellets is easy to use and many are certified organic. Best applied between February and the end of the growing season in October, pellets are rich in organic matter and nutrients and will help enrich the soil and maintain its balance. The recommended 'dosage' is 50 g (a scant 2 oz) per square metre.

I always use chicken pellets on the allotment – I just scatter them down the row. (Mike Wiffen)

Grow your own

An allotment is an ideal place to grow green manure, a fast-growing leafy crop – often a legume whose root nodules have the advantage of fixing nitrogen into the soil – which is then dug straight into the ground. As well as improving soil fertility green manures, especially autumn-sown ones, are good at mopping up the nutrients remaining after crops have been harvested, and help to prevent them being washed away by rain. On the minus side they are highly attractive to slugs.

You need at least a six-week 'window' to make green manure, and this is a reasonable timetable.

- **Summer:** buckwheat and fenugreek if you have room. These are good for smothering weeds but leave the soil very dry.

- **Late summer:** (before mid September): radish, mustard, alfalfa. Dig in by the end of October, or leave to get frosted over the winter.

- **September:** ryegrass. This will grow well all winter, can be dug in during spring and will release nutrients as it rots down. Usually very hardy, their frosted remains can be left as a mulch.

Sowing green manure seeds is easy – just broadcast them by the handful and rake them into the soil then dig them in when they are lush and leafy. (Ruth)

Except for clovers, whose flowers attract helpful insect pollinators, green manures are best dug in before they flower. Then allow at least two weeks, if not more, before sowing crop seeds. If the weather is very dry the leaves may take up to a month to rot fully.

The wormery

If you are easily able to take your kitchen waste to the allotment a wormery is another way of making compost. It will also accommodate some – but not too many – grass cuttings. Rather than solid compost the wormery produces a concentrated liquid feed, which is drained off from the bottom of the composter, as well as solid 'black gold'. The average wormery contains around 500 worms, which work their way up through a series of trays.

> I gained a big reputation as an eccentric, thanks to the wormery! First problem: find your worms. The books tell you to buy them at a fishing bait shop, of which there is a dearth in Highgate. I eventually solved the problem when I realized that the little red worms in my maturing heap of manure were exactly the worms required. I then took home several sacks of manure, spread it out on the patio, and spent some happy hours collecting the worms, much to the disgust of my family!
>
> The wormery worked well in the summer and autumn, though I never quite got the hang of how much food they could deal with. But when winter came there was a big problem of insulation. I could have bought something, but in the end it was easier to just take the worm container home and install it in a corner of our large kitchen/living room. It caused a few raised eyebrows but worked well. It only smelled when I took the lid off and the important thing was that the worms seemed happy and carried on the good work. (Alexa Stace)

What to do with manure – and when

> Horse manure needs to be two or three years old to be any good. (Doug Chainey)

There are those who like to dig in manure in spring and others who favour spreading a layer of manure over the plot in the autumn and letting the worms and bacteria, with the help of the weather, decay it enough so that it can be lightly forked in spring. This is fine as long as your manure is really well rotted. If it's not, you'll find you have big lumps left which are hard to rake out and will make the ground unsuitable for root crops like parsnips. Digging manure in during the autumn may help it rot but, particularly if your soil is fine and chalky, winter rain may leach out a lot of the nutrients.

When we've done a spring treatment we've dug trenches and heaved in manure by the forkful. It is tricky for root crops, so we set aside an area to treat later in the year. We feed that with the fine, concentrated stuff. (Ruth)

Fruit bushes, especially shallow-rooted ones like raspberries and strawberries, as well as rhubarb which is a notoriously greedy feeder, will appreciate a manure mulch in late winter or early spring, well before they start into growth.

Compost

Fine, really well-rotted compost can be sieved to make a good potting medium, either on its own or mixed with a proprietary (ideally peat-free) brand. Like manure, compost can be used on the surface or dug in, and is a better top dressing for crops like asparagus. Light compost, either home-made or concentrated, is an ideal late-winter treatment for perking up overwintered crops like sprouting broccoli, cabbages and garlic. Later in the year, you can use it around leeks, courgettes and brassicas.

SOWING AND PLANTING

Although not the purists' choice, it is perfectly acceptable to buy (or accept from a friend) ready-grown vegetable plants and put them in your plot, to grow onions from sets and to start asparagus from ready-grown crowns. However, just about every allotment vegetable can be grown from seed if you have the time and the inclination.

Choosing seed

When you are buying seed, look to see whether varieties are labelled 'F1'. If F1 they will be more expensive, and there will be fewer seeds per packet because they will be the result of first-generation crosses bred to emphasize some particular characteristic such as disease resistance or early cropping. 'Ordinary' seed is better value and often just as easy to grow, so it is worth experimenting to see which you prefer and which does best in your plot. If you like to keep seed from one year to the next – runner and French beans, for example – remember that seeds from F1 varieties are not guaranteed to come true.

I always send away for my seeds. They're expensive but you get the variety. (Mike Wiffen)

You may also want to look for organic seeds and for old 'heritage' seeds and for foreign varieties such as French and Italian. Every year new and exotic vegetables come onto the market. The choice is yours.

I liked to find special varieties you couldn't get at ordinary nurseries. (Pat Bence)

Straight in the plot

Even if you are planning to transplant seedlings they can be started in an area (or several small ones) you have set aside as a seedbed. To get the fine soil you need it may help to sieve it, and mix it with some fine peat-free potting compost before you sow. Scatter the seeds over a small area and cover them with soil, or use successive parts of a row to raise seeds. A covering of fleece, cloche or equivalent will add warmth and get seeds off to a good start.

Any vegetables – such as parsnips – that don't like being moved, need to be sown straight into the allotment soil and thinned later. (Ruth)

Even if you are sowing in a block, it helps to use a line to hand to ensure straight rows. Planting by eye is fine for sowings such as small patches of radishes or lettuce seeds that will later be transplanted.

As a rule, the larger the seed the more deeply it needs to be planted. For small seeds like leeks and rocket a good method is to make a shallow furrow with the end of a trowel or dibber, sprinkle in the seeds and cover them lightly with soil. Seed packets usually give a recommended planting depth on the back.

Always water the drill before sowing. Watering from above forms a hard crust over the seeds and makes it difficult for them to push through. (Tim Callard)

The biggest problem with small seeds is to get them planted sparsely enough. One trick I've discovered is to mix the seed with a handful of fine soil or sand before you plant. (Ruth)

You can buy a gadget marketed as a 'Pro-Seeder' that adjusts to seed size and dispenses them at the right distance.

For larger seeds, like peas and beans, you can either make a deeper trench for planting or place seeds into individual holes made with a pointed trowel or dibber.

After you've finished your sowing, don't forget to label what you've planted. Seeds will need a gentle watering in (too much pressure will dislodge them) and protecting from slugs and snails – and other pests like birds and rabbits – which can munch off the tops as soon as they appear. To help seeds to get started quickly you may also want to cover them with cloches, polythene or fleece.

In the early allotment years we often planted seeds then accidentally trod on the area afterwards. We quickly devised a system of making string 'fences' around the planted areas – that's what we always use now. (Ruth)

If seeds don't come up, you can just start again. Even planted late they will almost certainly catch up. It may have been too cold for them, seedlings may have been eaten before you could get to see them, or it may just have been poor seed.

Pots, trays and cells

An allotment neighbour introduced me to cells – since then I've never looked back. (Ruth)

Many vegetables do best raised from seed at home then planted out into the allotment once well established. When you are using containers, sow small seeds thinly, and bigger ones either singly or in pairs. To get vibrant root systems going you need containers that are good and deep. Pots are fine (with crocks added for good drainage), but for bigger seeds, cells are ideal. These hinged containers, which pack into a plastic frame, come apart easily for removing established plants.

To avoid running out of containers we collect deep plastic containers from the supermarket to use for raising seeds. The best ones already have holes stamped in the bottom. After planting, covering them in cling film gets them going fast. (Ruth)

To prevent seeds and seedlings getting overwet and dying from rot, a mixture of potting compost and vermiculite (ratio 70:30 approximately) makes a great growing medium because it maximizes drainage. You can use an all-purpose compost or a special seed compost – both are fine.

Before being put out into the plot, seedlings may need to be thinned in their containers by removing the weakest. They may also need potting on. A kitchen fork or pointed 'mini trowel' is handy for getting them out when you do this. Be sure to check both roots and shoots when selecting the healthiest seedlings. If you've begun the seeds in a specialist compost such as John Innes No. 1 you will need to upgrade at this point.

Hardening off

When seedlings of tender plants are raised indoors they need hardening off before they can be planted out. If you have a cold frame, keep it open during the day and close it at night. If you don't you will have to carry pots and trays outdoors in the morning and bring them indoors again in the evening. Watch out for slugs and snails, which can quickly converge on tender crops, especially in the last stage of hardening off when seedlings are left outdoors all night.

It was a tray of healthy, really good-looking cucumber plants. Once they were accidentally left outside the front door, by a flower bed, overnight. Of the nine seedlings, three had been seriously attacked next morning; the trails were added evidence of mollusc guilt. (Ruth)

Planting out

You can never get the space right. I always put rows wide apart and then they fill in. (Robin Barrett)

At the allotment, the guidelines for straight rows, labels and protection are much as for seed planting. Otherwise, make sure the soil is good and damp. For leafy, thirsty plants like brassicas and lettuces, pouring water into individual planting holes before inserting plants is essential:

Puddling in is a must – particularly for Brussels sprouts and when raising any brassicas. There's no other way to get them going. (Chris Luck)

You may also want to add a handful of concentrated manure in each hole. Give plants plenty of space, too.

When planting out, we have got into the habit of popping in a few 'spares' at the end of a row of sprouts or leeks. When these flourish (as they usually do) we are notoriously reluctant to take them out, but bunches of leek 'spares' have flavoured some of the best allotment soups. (Ruth)

Rows or blocks?

The allotment tradition is for planting in rows, but even without raised beds planting in half rows or small blocks is a good idea. Growing plants like lettuces in a block can help reduce weeds and improve water retention. For some crops, such as sweetcorn, a block is also essential to ensure fertilization.

Whatever your choice, make sure that large plants like brassicas have enough room to grow to maturity without competing with their neighbours for light and root room. Good spacing will also allow air to circulate and prevent the over-humid conditions in which diseases like downy mildew thrive. A useful space-saving tip is to stagger plants to maximize the space between them. You also need to make sure that you have enough space to weed properly between plants without trampling on your precious crops and to harvest with ease.

Our five-rod Dorset allotment is long and thin, with a path down the middle. On either side we plant either in rows or, for crops we want to grow in smaller amounts, like rocket and radicchio, in blocks. (Ruth)

Sowing in succession

For allotment vegetables and herbs that mature quickly – which includes everything from lettuce, radishes and spinach to beetroots, beans, peas, dill and coriander – it is sensible to aim to sow small amounts of seed in succession, so as to extend the harvest time of the crop. This works fine most of the time, but if early sowings get a slow start and later ones motor on more quickly than planned you can still end up with everything maturing at the same time. A lot depends on the weather in any particular season.

WATER AND WATERING

However much you water, the rain always does the job best. (Ruth)

An allotment without water on tap can be a nightmare unless you live almost next door to your allotment, and can run a hose to your plot. However, with ingenuity there are ways and means of getting water to a plot if you really have to.

A really nice neighbour put a tap in the side of his house, next to the allotment. That's a real, real bonus. (John Makin)

Without such luck, allotmenters without water available have to resort to other methods.

Within days of getting the allotment, water was pouring from a broken drain across the road; lorries hissed noisily through it for three weeks, damp ran across the road outside the allotment gate – no way could we harvest it. Then it was winter, a wildlife pond was dug, the first watering cans carried 200 yards from home to allotment. (How had we not noticed it was uphill?) A cheap trolley holding four large containers was a relative breakthrough but not an answer. Finally, an institutional neighbour gave us permission to fill the pond with a hosepipe from its tap – and the buses/lorries didn't puncture the hosepipe. (Hendrina Ellis)

It was a dry spring, more water was needed – the trolley collapsed under the load and son returned to university. Back shamefacedly to loading the boot of the car, but without son can only fill containers part way. Son's eyes glaze as they realise that enthusiastic exchange of news is always followed by request for 'just a hand with the water'. We get by. (Hendrina Ellis)

There are other ways of getting around the problem:

Some people used to come with a Land Rover and they had huge five-gallon or more containers which they filled up with water from the tap in the churchyard. They would then drive up to their plot, stick a hose in and siphon off what they wanted from their container. (Robin Barrett)

Or the weather may be on your side:

We don't have taps but God has provided plenty of water – we are in Wales! Everyone has water butts and they say it's no problem. It's just a question of catching it. (Ann Tucker)

On tap

Allotments need a lot of water and most of it's yours – not rain. (Damien Grove)

Water is usually supplied to allotments either via taps (ideally placed strategically over tanks) or self-fill tanks from which you scoop water with a can. The number of plots per tap or tank will vary from site to site, but one for four plots is about average.

Dedicated allotment gardeners will do all they can to reduce the need for watering with ruses such as this:

I have an area about 5 ft by 5 ft where I dig out the soil completely down to an orangey clay base (about a spit and a bit). Then I fill it up with lumpy manure and the returned soil. I then cover that with carpet, cut a hole in it, plant courgettes – and forget them. I don't water them at all. I've done that for two years now, otherwise you're watering all the time. You need some sort of base. If I was on looser soil I'd use a plastic liner. (Chris Luck)

If you are allowed to hose, consider the needs of your neighbours, as this cautionary tale illustrates:

One very hot summer the need for water almost turned into a war. Someone with two large plots, both full of tomatoes and other thirsty crops, would commandeer the taps and have his hoses on for hours, deaf to the pleas of his neighbours. It seemed impossible to outwit him and only the diplomatic intervention of the committee chairman stopped the situation developing into fisticuffs. Since he was retired and able to be at the allotment all day, every day, he was persuaded to hose early on so that people who worked could do their watering in the evening. He did grow the most fantastic vegetables. (Ruth)

Given the need for water conservation, many allotments frown on – or even ban – the use of sprinklers, so check before you get into trouble. And because it can take several hours for a sprinkler to wet the plot thoroughly, this can be another way of infuriating your neighbours.

Even when there are water taps available, and certainly when water has to be carried some distance in cans, the 'green' and savvy plot holder will try to find some way of collecting rainwater. The ideal, if it can be managed, is to run water from a piece of guttering on the shed roof into a water butt, but even an open tank to collect rainwater is better than nothing (though it will take up valuable space on a small plot).

There are other ways of cutting down the legwork. A neighbour on our Dorchester site has installed a huge water container next to his plot which, with ingenuity, he has managed to fill and refill with a hose. No more trailing of cans for him. (Ruth)

Equipment

Watering cans – ideally, two per person if you have to carry water far – are essential. A wheelbarrow can also be useful:

I've pioneered the wheelbarrow approach. You can fit four watering cans in these. If it sloshes inside you can just tip it out onto the plot. (Sue Bryant)

If you are allowed a hose, it helps to have a hose reel with a handle too, which will help stop it kinking – and, inevitably, perishing in the places where it has bent – as well as saving energy. You need an attachment that will fit snugly onto the tap provided; an adjustable metal ring that you can tighten with a screwdriver is helpful. Your chosen nozzle should give you everything from a fine spray to a jet.

Good watering timing and technique can help make best use of your energy and the precious liquid.

Good watering tips

When the weather is hot, watering is best done in the evening or, even better, early in the morning to cut down the amount of evaporation from the soil and water loss (transpiration) from plants, though you will probably have to work around the other demands on your time.

Water well. It can be as damaging and stressful to plants to give them just a sprinkling of water as none at all.

> *Water needs to soak down to lower levels to ensure deep rooting. You need at least 2 gallons per square yard. [However,] peas and beans are best kept on the dry side until they flower. Then they need a thorough watering. But never let vegetables grown for their leaves dry out. (Tim Callard)*

Don't water too much – give plants a chance to put down deep roots and establish themselves well. Overwatering can also encourage wilt and other fungal diseases.

Water right to the roots rather than spraying water onto the leaves.

> *For plants sensitive to cold, such as tomatoes, cucumbers, aubergines and peppers, always use water from a butt which is warm. (Tim Callard)*

Give extra attention to shallow-rooted plants and those like cucumbers whose fruit has a high water content.

Use a fine spray on seedlings so that you don't dislodge their roots.

Plant thirsty, short-lived plants like lettuces close together.

Use fleece over plants, especially in windy weather, to cut down water loss.

When transplanting, pour water into each individual planting hole to give the roots maximum moisture and minimize slowdown in growth.

> *Water transplants little and often until they are established. This can be twice a day in hot spells. (Tim Callard)*

If you have young fruit trees, sink watering spikes next to them, and give water as directly to the roots as possible.

Be careful of watering in the evening if it is likely to be frosty. You may kill plants by icing up their roots.

Health warning

Don't use your allotment water tank for washing out a spray or can that has had weedkiller in it. You risk killing other people's crops as well as your reputation. The same is true if you are using insecticide – particularly as your neighbours may be growing organically.

Weedkiller got into the self-filling tanks we use for watering. Understandably there were glum faces and angry words exchanged around the site and warnings subsequently posted. (Ruth)

FOOD FOR PLANTS

Good compost should provide most of the nutrients plants need, but many will benefit from extra feeding, especially during peak growing times. Without enough food they not only fail to grow well but have poor disease resistance. Some allotment vegetables, including tomatoes, leeks and onions, sprouts, cabbages and cauliflowers, are notoriously greedy feeders so will need special attention. Another reason why plants may need extra feed is to provide them with small amounts of vital trace elements that are essential to their health.

Rather than buying ready-made feed, here is a good way of making a liquid fertilizer. Fill a cotton shoe bag with compost and soak it in a bucket of water for about a week, jigging it around every few days to mix it well. The rich brown liquid you get can then be watered direct onto plants.

There are other ways of feeding plants, like this ingenious solution for tomatoes.

My friend cuts the bottom off a lemonade bottle and inserts it at the base of a tomato plant. First she puts some stones in and then a handful of chicken pellet manure. With the stones in there, water doesn't drain through too quickly. The chicken pellets dissolve over about a week and feed the plants. (Maureen Nightingale)

The amount of extra food you need to provide depends greatly on the type of soil you have in your allotment. Plants growing in fast-draining chalk and sand are likely to need much more food than those on clay.

After London clay, on which most things seemed to do well without more than compost and a little blood and bone meal, Dorset chalk was a bit of a shock. The first year's Brussels sprouts were especially poor, but we soon discovered, as one allotment neighbour (and show winner) confirmed, that you have to 'feed, feed, feed' to get anything worthwhile. The more the soil is composted the better it gets, but the nutrients still leech out incredibly quickly. (Ruth)

Extra feeds: choice and application

The extra feed you give your plants can be organic or inorganic but the better your soil is in the first instance the less feed you will have to give.

SOOT AND WOOD ASH

If you have a coal or wood burning fire at home you may want to save soot and ashes to put on the garden. These are fine, but not complete foods by any means.

I asked a visiting allotment judge about using soot as a fertilizer – he said keep it for three years and then spread it lightly over the soil – it provides some nutrients and it keeps the slugs and snails at bay. (Andrew Malleson)

ORGANIC OR INORGANIC?

While organic fertilizers come from purely natural sources, inorganic ones are manufactured from a mixture of chemicals, many of which are derived ultimately from naturally occurring rocks. The choice is yours.

Organic is the thing – it's going back to the old ways of doing things. (Sue Bryant)

FISH, BLOOD AND BONE MEAL

These good old-fashioned organic fertilizers are excellent applied at the beginning of the growing season as they release their goodness slowly over the season. As a guide, allow about 120–180 g (4–6 oz) per square metre (square yard).

SEAWEED

Seaweed is high in trace elements, but in its 'raw' form is too salty to use in the allotment. If collected from the top of the beach you need to leave it out to get rinsed by the rain for at least a month before putting it on the compost heap. It can be bought in a granular form and, as such, makes an excellent top dressing.

Ready-prepared

If you choose ready-prepared mixtures, be sure to dilute and/or apply them strictly according to the manufacturer's instructions. Generally, these work fast, and should only be used just before and during the growing season.

Feeds applied as powder or granules direct to the soil rather than being watered in are best forked in very lightly or left as a top dressing. If you put them on when the ground is wet they will get to plant roots most quickly. Never let granulated fertilizer come into direct contact with plants as it can scorch and damage them, and take care to sprinkle them as evenly as possible. Keep them well away from soil in which you are going to plant or have planted seeds and don't be tempted to add more than the recommended amount. Overfeeding, especially of vegetables such as beans, can stimulate them to make leaves in preference to fruits.

To get food directly and quickly to plants foliar feeding is an ideal method, although not a substitute. Foliar feeds come in both organic and non-organic (inorganic) forms; as always, follow the maker's instructions.

Special feeds are formulated for specific plants such as tomatoes, usually in liquid form. If you don't want to buy these, you can also make your own from nettles or comfrey.

What feeds contain

With all feeds, the symbols you need to take notice of are NPK – which stand for nitrogen, phosphates and potassium. A good all-purpose fertilizer will contain them in the proportions of 18 nitrogen to 8 phosphate and 8 potassium and will also note the presence of magnesium and other trace elements.

Nitrogen: vital to all plants with green leaves such as spinach and cabbage.

Phosphates: improve the general health of plants as well as stimulating the growth of roots and the development of flowers vital to crops such as peas and beans.

Potassium: helps to improve resistance to pests and diseases as well as promoting the production of flowers and development of fruits. Wood ash from a bonfire is a good source of potassium.

Magnesium: essential for the production of the green pigment chlorophyll in plant leaves.

Manganese: often lacking in sandy and alkaline soils. Necessary for making healthy, green, long-lasting leaves and for the formation of roots in crops like beetroot and parsnips.

Iron: lack of iron hinders good leaf formation. It is most usually a problem on alkaline, limey soils.

Molybdenum: also key to good leaf formation, particularly in brassicas.

Boron: essential for root vegetables which without it turn brown and crack. Also needed by brassicas such as cauliflowers. If necessary add borax, mixed with sand or soil, at 30 g (1 oz) per 20 square metres (20 square yards).

Zinc: boosts plant vigour.

Copper: helps harden leaf surfaces, making them more resistant to pests and diseases.

PLANT PROTECTION

Plants need protection mainly to prevent attacks from pests and to speed seed germination and plant growth. With the added warmth that cloches, cold frames, fleece and polytunnels provide you can have vegetables really early in the season, and even without a greenhouse you have the chance to grow heat-loving crops like peppers, chillis and melons.

Although they will not give you full frost protection, these coverings also allow you to overwinter plants grown from seed in the autumn to give you a head start the following spring, or to harden off tender plants raised at home. Early in the year, cloches, fleece and tunnels can be used to help warm up the soil before planting. At the end of the season, after bad weather or before the start of the new one, give all your cloches a good wash to let in as much light as possible.

Cold frames

The cold frame is essentially a mini unheated greenhouse with a roof that opens to allow for watering and temperature regulation. You can buy frames ready made – from posh hardwood glazed versions to metal frames covered in polythene. Or, if you are handy at DIY, you could try constructing one yourself.

> *The best lettuces ever were planted out in a moveable metal frame with spiked feet that stuck into the ground. It came originally with a polythene covering that only lasted a couple of years before it got torn to shreds. Using the wrapping from a double mattress we cut new pieces to fit the sides and another to go from back to front that could be secured with a couple of bricks when the frame was closed or rolled back to keep it open. By saving any likely polythene whenever we acquired it the frame lasted years but unfortunately was abandoned when we eventually had to leave the plot. (Ruth)*

Cloches

Traditionally made from glass, most cloches sold now are of clear plastic. The oldest sorts are bell-shaped covers for one large or a few small plants. You need to be able to lift and move cloches easily for watering and weeding, but they also need to be held in place firmly enough that they're not blown away at the first spring gale. When not in use, they are best stored in a shed.

> *We have a selection of corrugated plastic cloches in frames inherited from my father. They work OK, but it means being assiduous about watering. They are particularly good for bringing on brassica seedlings, basil and early and late lettuces. (Ruth)*

The best cloches come with 'feet' to keep them secure and vented ends that can be opened or closed. You can make cloches yourself from hoops of wire with sheets of corrugated polythene slatted through, or look out for purpose-made wire frames – they are hard to find new but turn up at places like car boot sales and village fetes. With this arrangement you may want to add at least one 'end', for which you will need some extra rigid polythene and sticks to keep the ends in place. Small pieces to half the cloche height will keep off the worst of the weather and allow some ventilation.

For protecting individual plants when they are small, an economical way of making cloches is to cut the bottoms off plastic drinks bottles and use these. They need some air holes spiked in the top with a skewer or sharp knife.

Fleece

Fleece has the advantage of letting in both air and rain, which can be a boon if you are not able to water every day. In dry weather fleece also helps to slow evaporation. But peg it down well – it easily gets blown off by the wind.

> *We always have fleece on something – and in winter it is great for keeping things like beetroot from getting frosted. When it gets tatty at the edges we cut it down into smaller pieces, but you do eventually have to get new. We made our own pegs from pieces of thick wire bent with pliers. They are much better than the thick plastic ones. (Ruth)*

You can buy fleece by the metre or opt for a ready-made fleece tunnel complete with a metal frame and drawstring ends. Because fleece gets damaged easily, you need to be prepared to renew it once it gets past its best. If you're in a hurry, you can water plants gently through fleece (in imitation of rain) but ideally it's best to lift up the fleece (when you can also do some weeding) and water plants direct to the roots. Even if you mainly use the tunnels it's handy to have some lengths of fleece in the shed to cut to size and put over plants on an *ad hoc* basis if frosts are threatened.

> *Radish perfection. As well as helping to raise a really early first crop, I always put radishes under fleece to help keep off flea beetles. The warmth and moisture make for tender, juicy radishes at high speed. Unbeatable. (Ruth)*

Polytunnels

These are also available as ready-cut sheets and wire frames to fit, and with enough polythene supplied to tie and secure at the tunnel ends. Like fleece, the polythene does not last indefinitely and will need to be replaced periodically. They can also get blown away, however. The very smallest polytunnels, which are cloche size (they are sold by some suppliers as 'sectional tunnel cloches') have hinged frames that allow them to fold flat when not in use.

Netting

Why is it that we always seem to need to put up netting on the windiest of days? I hate the stuff. (Ruth)

Fine mesh – 5 mm or less – is excellent for keeping off pests. On exposed allotment sites, it provides shade from the extremes of the sun, which is helpful for young crops, and helps to prevent the soil from drying out too quickly. Only the very finest mesh, however, will act as an effective barrier against carrot fly; it is sold under trade names such as 'Enviromesh'. It can be pinned to a wooden frame or used over the hoops you use to support fleece or polythene.

Wider mesh netting is fine for protecting crops from birds. It is perfectly all right draped over – and tied to – canes but for a really neat finish it needs to be attached to a proper frame. You can make one of these yourself from 2 x 2 timber (ideally treated to make it weatherproof) or build a frame using bought ball-shaped 'joints' into which you push metal or wooden rods. There is just about every level and quality of frame available, depending on what you can afford.

I have a purpose-built fruit cage – it's much quicker. I take the top netting off in the winter. The top netting overhangs the strawberries as well. (Edward Probert)

Netting will get hitched on any button, but especially those on the back pockets of shorts or trousers. I can't think how many times I've found myself unhitching netting that's got caught up that way. (Ruth)

Wide 15-mm netting makes a general-purpose protection for vulnerable plants like brassicas.

You don't even need to have it trailing right down to the ground for it to deter birds, though it is remarkable how cabbage white butterflies manage to find their way through it.

WEEDS AND WEEDING

It's a very weedy allotment really, but as soon as I see a weed he's out. I'm always hoeing. (Doug Chainey)

Dealing with weeds is a necessary allotment chore, but immensely satisfying. Getting rid of them is essential not only to allotment tidiness but also to plant health. As they grow, weeds take goodness from the soil and if close to crops can entwine stems and roots, so further restricting growth. Unlike enclosed gardens, allotments are open and extremely vulnerable to weed seeds blowing in on the wind. If there is just one uncultivated, weed-ridden plot nearby you are likely to be particularly at risk. Add to this the fact that allotment paths are often vegetated by grass and other vigorous perennials and your chances of keeping the allotment free of weeds is even further reduced.

With the onset of warmer winters, weeds now seem to grow most of the year, so weeding is a constant chore.

You winter dig and the weeds keep growing with our climate change. (Sue Bryant)

However, there are times of the year when weeding is essential:

You have to get on top of the weeds. May and the end of the season are critical. You don't want them to go to seed. (Tim Pryce)

And if you're really keen, even having one hand out of action needn't hold you back.

After an operation on one hand I used to do all my weeding with one hand, and with a basket on the other arm. You do if the passion is there. (Maureen Nightingale)

In spring, annual weeds have the nasty habit of springing into life at exactly the same time as the seeds you've planted, and it's not always easy to tell which is which. There are ways around the problem:

Last year I had weeds that look just like parsnips. In fact I was so overcome with weeds that I planted parsnips and beetroot in plugs so that I could tell which was which. (Tim Pryce)

As you clear your plot you'll get the feel of the weeds that are likely to be most troublesome. Even if you decide to use a weedkiller such as glyphosate on the plot before you begin cultivation there may well be areas – such as under fruit bushes you have inherited – that are almost impossible to treat in this way.

Types of weed

Weeds come in two sorts, annual and perennial. The annuals are relatively easy to control, especially if you are able to hoe and weed regularly. If you uproot as many as possible before they set seed you will see the benefits as the years go by. Common allotment annual weeds include hairy bitter cress, chickweed, groundsel, sow thistles, speedwell, scarlet pimpernels and many others. They are characterized by producing many small seeds, which germinate rapidly, especially when the soil surface is dampened by rain.

Perennial weeds are a menace because they spread both by seeds and by other means, including underground runners (modified stems) or rhizomes (modified roots), which can often penetrate as much as a metre (3 ft) below ground.

I've got a wonderful crop of convolvulus on my plot. It's all got a bit on top of me this year. (Reg Simmons)

There are two kinds of bindweed. One has relatively shallow thick white roots and big white flowers. They are quite easy to get rid of. Then there is the other kind – deeper with a network of roots which come up in clumps. That stuff is so deep rooted. The only way I've got rid of it is to dig right down to 2 feet or more.

It's a slow task. I've done this prior to planting raspberries and asparagus so I've had to invest a lot of time on that. (Edward Probert)

Many of these weeds will grow from tiny pieces of root and rhizome, making them virtually impossible to eradicate. Constant weeding should weaken them a little, but if you are loath to use weedkiller you may just have to persist.

Know your weeds: some common weeds and the way they multiply

Weed	Means of reproduction
Dandelion	Seeds and pieces of the long tap root
Dock	Seeds and pieces of root
Convolvulus (bindweed)	Creeping deep-set rhizomes
Creeping buttercup	Seeds and runners
Creeping thistles	Seeds and rhizomes
Ground elder	Shallow, rampant rhizomes
Nettle	Seeds and rhizomes
Horsetail	Spores and deep-set rhizomes
Couch grass	Seeds and rhizomes

In all our allotments we have been plagued by convolvulus. It has grown in strawberries and raspberries, under gooseberries, up asparagus – in fact almost everywhere you can imagine. We dig it out constantly. (Ruth)

Every gardener has their 'worst weed', and a way of combating it:

We have ground elder – you could throttle those monks for introducing that for their medicines. It took over. (Sue Bryant)

Horsetails are a pain – if you're a good gardener you keep on top of them. Their roots are black and deep and it's said that they bring treasure (and minerals) up to the surface. (Sue Bryant)

Weeding

Everyone develops their own weeding technique but, whatever works for you, be sure that you do not risk treading on your crops as you go.

I'm better off on my knees – I have back trouble so it's more comfortable. (Sue Bryant)

If the soil looks dry, it is wise to water before you weed (take off the top surface of the soil with a trowel first to see if it's damp beneath). A long-handled hoe is good for getting at small weeds between rows, but you may need to go over the area afterwards and pick off by hand any that look as if they may re-root. To get close to plants without damaging them you need a short-handled hoe, a trowel or a fork (either a hand fork or a regular one) as well as nimble fingers.

I've often found myself on all fours tackling weeds under fruit bushes or between asparagus. You have to be careful under the gooseberries. (Ruth)

To save wear and tear on your back, get down on your knees for close weeding and use a kneeling mat if that helps. As with digging, keeping a bucket close by you saves energy and helps to make sure that all weeds can be properly disposed of. After you have finished, especially if you have been weeding between small plants, take the precaution of watering well.

Other good tips for coping with weeds

- For very fine weeding, as between carrots, use a knitting needle.
- Mark rows of seeds with a line and hoe to within 25 mm (1 in) of this before seeds germinate.
- Resist hoeing when the soil is wet – you risk transplanting weeds from one part of the plot to another.
- Hoe and/or fork your weeds several times before raking over a patch of ground where you will sow seeds or set plants.
- Weed and thin at the same time when dealing with crops like lettuce, parsnips and beetroot.

Suppressing weeds

Keeping weeds in the dark will help to prevent them growing and spreading. To do this you can cover weedy areas with carpet or thick black polythene, though this is not guaranteed to get rid of persistent offenders like couch grass and horsetails, even after a year.

We put carpets down – used in the right way they are good, but lots of sites are banning them because people leave them too long. They need to be just on the surface, and if weighted down they are great. It's got to be carpet with a woven back – a good old piece like Axminster or Wilton – not the foam type. (Sue Bryant)

Mulching will also help to deprive weeds of light. A mulch can be organic, in the form of bark or compost, or you can buy and lay sheets of black matting, which is ideal for keeping weeds from ruining an area such as a strawberry bed. The best way of using this matting is to weed thoroughly, lay it, then cut holes in it through which plants are inserted.

A traditional way of getting rid of annual weeds and even suppressing perennials is to plant potatoes. Or you can put in a quick-maturing crop of green manure. Growing flowers may also help, because chemicals exuded by the roots of one plant restrict the growth of a neighbour. That is why you should plant nasturtiums to help kill couch grass and marigolds to get rid of ground elder and bindweed.

I grow Mexican marigolds, Tagetes minuta, which is supposed to hold the baddies at bay; it keeps back ground elder which doesn't like its root secretions. It grows to 6 ft high and the smell is fantastic, but I can't get it to flower as yet. (Sue Bryant)

Weedkillers

If you are going to use weedkiller on your allotment, then your best choice is one containing the biodegradable chemical glyphosate. This works systemically, being transported from leaves to roots. It is best applied in dry weather and you need to allow a couple of weeks for it to work completely. If spraying could risk damaging fruit or vegetable plants you may be able to dab it onto plants direct, but be sure to do this on a calm day and wear rubber gloves. If you can isolate weeds with a piece of paper or even, with convolvulus, get it to climb up a bamboo cane, then so much the better.

PESTS AND DISEASES

Hard as you try it seems impossible to avoid pests and diseases.

The bloke next door to me said, 'How's the allotment?' I said, 'Not too good. The peas have got moth, the onions have got mildew, the leeks have got leek moths and the potatoes have got the blight.' His reply was: 'Best you emigrate!' (Damien Grove)

Pests

Allotment pests come in many guises – large, small and virtually invisible. You will never be able to deter or exterminate them all, but you can at least try to minimize the damage they cause. Some pests are specific to particular vegetables and fruit (and are dealt with in that context), while others do their damage on a much wider scale.

RABBITS

Allotment rabbits will munch just about anything, though they don't much like strong-smelling vegetables such as onions and leeks. Overnight, rabbits can devastate a row of newly planted runner beans or parsley plants, or some nicely germinated carrot seedlings. They will even dig up and chew at parsnips, carrots or beetroot, or make tunnels to get at these sustaining crops.

While it is possible to protect individual rows or blocks of crops with netting, the only effective way of keeping rabbits off your plot is to surround it with a fence, which it may pay you to have installed professionally. In any event, do not underestimate rabbits' capabilities:

Last year, rabbits were even jumping the fences. (Doug Chainey)

The ideal rabbit-proof fence needs to be about 1 m (3 ft) high, made of wire mesh supported with stout posts. It also needs to be sunk well down, allowing about 30 cm (1 ft) of fencing below ground level. This can be tilted a little to add an extra deterrent. If you have a shed on your plot, make sure the netting goes right around its base – rabbits will happily shelter, or even 'nest' under a shed. To avoid having to climb over the fence all the time, it helps if you add at least one gate to the fence, or devise some sort of hinging mechanism to make it easy to get in and out.

> *For us, rabbits are a persistent problem, to the extent that frustrated plot holders have been known to take an air gun and shoot them at night. 'Bags' of a dozen and more have been reported. One plot holder even took farm ferrets with her to chase and catch them. Persistent nagging of the Council resulted in fencing around the allotment perimeter, which eased the problem a little, but we're sure that there are still rabbits strolling in through the open gate. (Ruth)*

DEER

Deer are a problem in some country allotments, but impossible to keep from individual plots except with very high fencing, and an issue for the owners or managers of your allotment site. Deer also carry ticks, the vectors of lyme disease, and this makes them a serious problem.

SQUIRRELS

These are most likely to be a pest if mature trees grow around or on your site. Protein-rich vegetables such as broad beans, peas and sweetcorn are their favourite foods, and you may need to protect these with netting barriers about 1 m (3 ft) tall, covered over the top. Growing in blocks, not rows, makes erecting such barriers much easier to manage.

> *Our sweetcorn had been eaten in an incident that was almost tremendously embarrassing. I was just about to go on the rampage, charging everyone – and then the traces became apparent. We put up a cage for it after that.*
> *(Anthony Pearson)*

MOLES

The last place you want to find molehills is in the middle of your plot, but if they live round about you may well be vulnerable. Unless you use traps, they are almost impossible to get rid of, and the more worms you have in your (healthy) plot the more they will like visiting.

*I generally catch between 20 and 30 moles a year. I put down traps, I'm afraid.
There's nothing worse than them coming up under your seedbed. (Doug Chainey)*

In the country there are as many remedies as there are gardens invaded by moles.

*They say you should make holes in the top of the molehills and put mothballs
down them, but I can't see those shifting this lot. (Michael Edwards)*

RATS AND MICE

Rats and mice can be a problem if they invade your sheds, and will use anything from newspaper to strawberry straw for bedding and eat any seeds or crops left in there (though they don't seem to like onions).

*Left lying on the shed floor, a pair of gardening gloves were chewed up by mice –
presumably for a nest. (Ruth)*

Mice will dig up and eat bean and pea seeds, especially if these are planted early in the year when there is little other food around. The old-fashioned way of deterring them is to lay branches of gorse or holly over the ground after planting, but fleece or netting well pegged down will do just as well, if not better. Keep an eye open for signs of small feet digging at your plantings, and if necessary be prepared to replant.

Mice also like root vegetables:

*The mice will get at your beetroot and make little holes in them if you leave
them in the ground. (Eric Sherwood)*

BIRDS

The pigeons will decapitate anything if they get the chance. (Anthony Pearson)

I use party poppers – that keeps the sparrows away. (Mike Wiffen)

I had lovely sweetcorn but it was all eaten by the magpies. (Tim Pryce)

Birds are beautiful creatures, but not welcome when they feed on your precious fruit and vegetables. Brassicas, especially when newly planted, are a magnet for pigeons, and blackbirds are chief among soft fruit lovers, particularly when the weather is dry and they are in need of fluids. Netting (see p. 80) is the best deterrent.

There's a scarecrow on a plot near ours which is so lifelike it always pulls me up short. (Ruth)

For protecting seeds, a less obtrusive way of keeping birds off is to weave string across the bed, supported by a series of sticks. Look around any allotment site and you will see all manner of bird scarers from scarecrows to old CDs hung from bean sticks, plastic strips and windmills that flap in the wind, to plastic bottles put over the tops of stakes. Whether any of them are actually effective is uncertain, though the last of these ideas is a handy safety measure against being spiked in the eye or face by a cane.

Using a somewhat motley collection of poles, tied together with string, and with rather smart black netting tied over, we managed to make an effective fruit cage covering black and red currants and some early raspberries. By overlapping the netting along the sides and tying them together loosely with string it was easy to release the few birds that managed to find their way in through the bottom and get caught. (Ruth)

SLUGS AND SNAILS

I've had snails climbing right to the top of my raspberries and even runner bean plants. Do they need oxygen at those heights? (Ruth)

Both these pests will ravage allotment plants but, of the two, slugs are the worst offenders, since they will attack plants both above and below ground. The wetter the weather (or the more assiduous your watering) and the younger, softer and juicier a leaf or fruit, the more likely it is to be attacked. Snails – notably over the winter – will congregate in the dark shelter provided behind anything from a plank of wood to the underside of a plant pot.

Benign snails? In late April I picked a spring cabbage with a good, firm head, and no obvious signs of damage to the leaves. Nestling within the outer leaves were 11 snails of different sizes, which had obviously done no damage to the plant. Their final destination was the compost bin. (Ruth)

It is all very well to advise that slugs and snails should be hand picked and destroyed – ideally at night by torchlight – but on an allotment, especially if you are unable to visit every day (or when it is dark), this is pretty nearly impossible. And in a wet summer they can get ever more voracious.

These latest slugs would eat anything. They stripped all the foliage from a complete row of my potatoes. Not only that, these slugs are not nocturnal. They would start crunching at 4.00 or 5.00 p.m. (Sue Bryant)

There are ways of deterring them, which may or may not be practicable, but you may need to resort to slug pellets.

I have to use slug pellets – they eat everything. (Doug Chainey)

If you do, the most acceptable sorts are those labelled as friendly to pets, birds and children. Best of all are the newest organic ones based on ferric phosphate. It is best to start with a small 'dose' and up it a little if necessary, rather than covering the ground with them.

Every time we use ground coffee I refill the pot with water and keep it. I then pour it around roots against slugs – it really works. (Mike Cosgrove)

Or you can negotiate help from other sources.

Bottles of 'slops' from your local innkeeper sunk into the ground get rid of slugs nicely. And what a lovely death for them, drowning in beer! One of our chaps on site was kind enough to bring me bottles of the stuff in the summer. (Sue Bryant)

An increasingly popular organic slug treatment is with nematode worms. You have to send off for the 'cultures' of these slug-devouring worms and use the preparation all in one go, though it will store perfectly well in the fridge for up to three weeks. The worms come in powder form which you dilute with water and apply with a watering can. Although expensive compared with slug pellets they have the advantage of being totally chemical free.

Slugs and snails can get everywhere:

Slugs were even inside the onions – they just hollowed an onion out.
(Ken Daniels)

Here are some other ways of coping with slugs and snails that are worth a try.

Plastic bottles placed over individual plants	Effective, but only practicable for a very small crop, and need to be removed for watering
Upturned grapefruit halves with holes cut in them	Good, but can look unsightly. They need to be strategically placed
Beer traps	Quickly attract the pests, but a bother to maintain
Gravel and glass chippings, and similar commercial products	Needed in large quantities, and right up to plant stems. Will not deter slugs below ground
Copper rings	Fine for a few individual plants such as tomatoes. Good around pots

CATERPILLARS

The caterpillars most likely to appear on your allotment are those of the cabbage white butterfly. Brassicas of all kinds – and nasturtiums – are their favourite foods. The striped caterpillars hatch from clusters of green eggs, usually laid on the undersides of the leaves. If you see the butterflies flitting round your crops, then watch out for the eggs and, if possible, rub them off with your hands. But be warned, this is a messy, smelly job for which it is best to wear disposable gloves. You can keep the butterflies at bay with fine netting but you still need to watch out for caterpillars.

Netting is a pain – but it does help keep the butterflies off the cabbages. But you need fine netting, otherwise it's no good. (Angela Downs)

On my father's allotment caterpillars were always a problem but I was paid extra pocket money for picking them off, collecting them in a jam jar then killing them in boiling water. Yuk! (Ruth)

If you have a bad infestation, then a spray of derris is effective or, if you are organic, a preparation containing either natural pyrethrins or the bacterium *Bacillus thuringiensis*.

Other caterpillars that attack brassicas, and which respond to the same treatment, are those of the cabbage moth. Green or yellowish brown in colour, they bore into the hearts of cabbages, but also attack crops like swedes and turnips.

Some caterpillars are burrowers. Those of codling moths tunnel into apples, pears and plums, making them inedible. Take steps to prevent the adults laying eggs by hanging in vulnerable trees traps baited with pheromones which will attract and capture the males, so preventing mating. To be effective, these traps need to go up in April.

Cutworms, the caterpillars of various moths, live below ground where they chew at the roots of lettuces and at crops like carrots and potatoes. At their worst they can gnaw through the bases of stems, severing them and stopping plant growth completely. The best way of deterring these pests, which flourish in the environment provided by weeds, is to keep your plot as weed free as possible.

To help control caterpillars, welcome to your plot birds like blue tits, which consume them by the hundred. If you have trees on the plot or nearby you may want to put up nesting boxes.

Caterpillars of rare and prized species warrant conservative treatment.

A couple of weeks ago I found an elephant hawk moth caterpillar. A friend is feeding it on leaves from her garden fuchsias until it turns into a chrysalis. (Maureen Nightingale)

APHIDS

These pests come in several guises – blackfly, greenfly and whitefly – but all do their damage by feeding on the sap of young shoots and leaves, so stunting plant growth. Also, they often leave a sticky, honey-like substance on foliage, making it virtually inedible. However effective you may be in attracting aphid-devouring ladybirds to the plot (they are particularly attracted to flowers, and like to lay their eggs on those of fennel or daisies and their relations) you may need to intervene.

A bad attack: one autumn the whitefly on purple sprouting broccoli and Brussels sprouts was so bad that just touching a leaf made clouds of insects fly up, getting in our hair and making us itch. We stripped off all the worst-affected leaves and sprayed the plants. We did get some smallish sprouts, but the purple sprouting revived well and, thanks to a cold winter, we picked a super crop for over a month in the following spring. (Ruth)

Spraying plants regularly with a solution of soapy water is a good way of killing aphids, or you can make a garlic spray by infusing half a dozen chopped garlic cloves in boiling water for 15 minutes, then straining off and cooling the liquid. If you have hoses on your plot, just a thorough wash down can help get rid of aphids as long as you get right to the leaf undersides. Be careful with the delicate growing tips of crops like broad beans which can be broken off by a powerful water jet. Another approach is to buy an organic oil-based treatment which works by impairing the insects' physiology, effectively blocking the pores through which they breathe. Proprietary garlic and pyrethrum sprays (both plants naturally contain large amounts of sulphur) are also effective and safe.

The best insecticide is detergent in a squirter. It will suffocate butterfly eggs. Blackfly don't like it either. (Mike Wiffen)

If you are growing organically you can buy live ladybird larvae which munch their way through aphids by the hundred and boost nature's resources.

If you wait for laydybirds to eat all the blackfly we get down here you'll be waiting till Christmas. (Mike Wiffen)

Companion planting can also help keep whitefly at bay, although there may be other complications.

I put calabrese between my rows of parsnips to keep off whitefly but the tops are so enormous they're restricting the calabrese from developing. And if I try to clear them the calabrese roots are disturbed. The only thing they're not getting is whitefly. (Chris Luck)

WIREWORMS

Potatoes, but also beetroot, carrots, celery and asparagus, are most vulnerable to wireworms.

When lifting a potato crop one year we saw these shiny, tough-skinned orange insects with stiff bodies protruding from holes in the tubers. We sorted through the best of the crop, keeping them for storing. The worst we put in the compost. In following years we took special care to choose varieties advertised as wireworm resistant. (Ruth)

These avid tunnellers are the larvae of the click beetle, which lays its eggs in May and June, usually amongst weeds. An old way of getting rid of them is to make wireworm traps – pieces of cut carrot or potato pushed into sticks and buried about 5–10 cm (2–4 in) below the surface of the ground, from the time potato tubers start to swell. Every couple of weeks you need to pull up the traps and dispose of the wireworms that will have been attracted to them. Pieces of cut potato work well, too.

If wireworms are a problem, harvest crops as soon as they are mature, rather than leaving them in the ground. Because wireworms can live in the ground for four years or more before metamorphosing into adults, another good method is to sow a crop of green manure, such as mustard, in late summer, adjacent to vulnerable crops. This will not only attract the wireworms but also give them sufficient food to speed their maturation.

FLEA BEETLES

When your allotment crops are prey to flea beetles, leaves of radishes, rocket, turnips, swedes and brassicas such as sprouts and cabbages become pock-marked with small holes in the leaves, which may then turn yellow. A heavy infestation will at best make plants look unsightly (especially salad rocket). At worst it will stunt and kill. Keeping the beetles off plants with fleece or very fine netting (as for carrot fly) will protect them when they are young and most vulnerable, and garlic spray is highly effective. However, ingenious gardeners have devised other ways of combating them:

> *Watch out for flea beetles and be prepared to attack. Get a piece of wood and coat it with grease. Walk along the row of plants with the wood just touching their tops. As you do this the beetles will jump up and get stuck on the grease. (Tim Pryce)*

CABBAGE ROOT FLY

The maggots of the cabbage root fly attack the roots of newly transplanted brassicas, particularly cabbages and cauliflowers, making them collapse and die. When you pull up the plants you can see the white grubs on the sorry stumps that remain. The best way of preventing attacks is to stop them getting to the soil surface to lay their eggs. You can do this by covering plants with fine netting or fleece or you can buy collars to put around the bases of plants while they are young and vulnerable. They need to be about 10 cm (4 in) square with a hole in the middle through which you can 'thread' the roots when planting. Cloches or large plastic bottles cut to size will have the same effect.

You can make collars for cabbages with pieces of cardboard or thick paper. They are good for protecting individual plants.

Diseases

> *Everything's got rust this year – it was so wet. (Sue Bryant)*

Allotment crops are prey to a whole range of diseases. The majority are caused by either fungi or viruses, but plants are also prey to bacterial infections. Often, diseases are spread by insects and other pests, and can be extremely persistent, lying dormant in the soil over the winter, ready to strike again in the warmth and wet of spring, when new shoots are beginning to establish themselves. Wet, warm summers also create the prime conditions in which diseases will thrive.

Crop rotation will help to keep diseases at bay, but good hygiene is also key. It is important to remove any infected plant material as soon as you spot it and to burn it if possible. On no account should it be put on the compost heap. Tell someone what it is before you dump it. If garden waste collected at your recycling centre is made into compost they may prefer your infected rubbish to go to landfill.

Bonfires are not encouraged on our plot so we usually bag up the infected material and take it to the landfill skip. (Ruth)

The following infections are those that affect more than one sort of plant. Those specific to a single crop are covered in individual entries.

FUNGAL INFECTIONS
The problems caused by many fungal infections are worse when the weather is cold and damp, which is why you need to be careful not to overwater. Because they reproduce by means of tiny spores, which are blown in on the air from neighbouring plots and can lie dormant in the soil for many years, fungal infections can be very difficult to eradicate.

Once blight starts blowing around the plot there's no escape. (Ruth)

There are various approved fungicides on the market; whichever you use you need to follow instructions carefully. If you are gardening organically, sulphur and Bordeaux mixture are both safe to use.

Mildew
Downy mildew is the pale grey fungus that infects leafy crops like brassicas, lettuce and spinach, causing a furry coating on leaf undersides and yellow patches on upper surfaces. Spraying with Bordeaux mixture is the best treatment, though not guaranteed to work in all circumstances.

Powdery mildew is most likely to affect your apples and gooseberries. As its name suggests, leaves become covered with a white, powdery mould, and they become distorted. Fruit fails to set or, if it does, becomes cracked and split, often with brown patches. Fortnightly spraying with Bordeaux mixture is the best treatment.

Club root

A soil-borne fungus is the cause of club root, which affects all members of the cabbage family (brassicas), including swedes and turnips. The classic symptoms are swollen, deformed roots and yellowed leaves that quickly wilt in fine weather. Since the fungus thrives in acid conditions, liming the soil before you plant, at about 20 g (6 oz) per square metre (square yard) will help achieve the ideal soil pH of around 7 to 7.5. Good drainage, aided by adding plenty of compost, will also help. At planting time, putting a little calomel dust in each planting hole can also help to deter this persistent disease. And make sure you rotate your crops well.

My father's allotment was plagued with club root but he swore by calomel dust. His cauliflowers were always huge. (Ruth)

Stem rot

This is a problem that mostly affects marrows, squashes and cucumbers, but also tomatoes. Despite its name the fungus responsible for this problem usually makes itself obvious by creating slimy brown patches on plant leaves, before it goes on to invade the stems. Left untreated, plants will shrivel and die.

Root rot

Above ground, the first signs of root rot are brown or yellow shrivelling stems. If the fungus has taken hold affected plants are likely to die rapidly and it is unlikely that you will be able to save them. All types of beans and peas, cucurbits and tomatoes are likely victims. There is little you can do except pull up and burn the plants or dispose of them safely. Ideally you should also remove the infected soil or, at the very least, leave it uncultivated for a year or two.

Brown rot

Tree fruits like apples, and many vegetables, including courgettes, marrows and broad, French and runner beans can be attacked by this fungus which lives up to its name by turning crops brown, but not before it has made itself visible as a cottony white mould on the stems, leaves and fruits. To prevent the infection lingering from year to year you need to avoid composting any infected plant material and, on fruit trees, use an approved fungicide early in the season to prevent the infection taking hold.

Damping off

This is a fungus that affects vegetable seedlings, making them keel over and die. Being sparing with water, and using sterilized pots and soil are the best ways of avoiding the problem.

In the early days I thought I was being good to my cucumber seeds by watering them well. Not a bit of it. No sooner had they come up than one by one they collapsed and died – damped off. I'm now really careful to water cucumbers and other seedling sparingly, testing the soil to make sure it is quite dry before watering. With seedlings being raised in pots, watering from below has also turned out to be the best way of keeping them healthy. (Ruth)

Rust

The rusts caused by fungi are most likely to affect members of the onion family (usually leeks and garlic) and also runner and French beans. Mint can also be attacked. Typical symptoms are yellow or orange pustules on leaves – hot, humid summers are their favourite growing conditions. As long as infection is mild, the best treatment is none at all, though you can try a sulphur-based fungicide. As long as plants survive, keep them well fed and watered and with luck they will recover.

It was a hot, dry summer and however much water we gave the leeks, and however well we mulched and fed them, nothing seemed to cure the rust. The worst we pulled up and burned, but the rest we left. Come the rains and cool of autumn and suddenly they burst back into life. By the spring, those we hadn't eaten were big and strong. In March there were three good enough to win second prize in the spring show. (Ruth)

Mint rust looks unsightly but is rarely fatal. If infection is bad, you may want to remove some pieces of root and replant them in a clean pot in sterile soil then burn the rest. When established they can be replanted in a different spot.

> *Infected allotment mint was certainly not good enough to use in the kitchen. But I cut off all the tops in early July and in a month had an excellent crop of fresh, new growth good enough to make the annual jars of mint sauce. (Ruth)*

Leaves of bean plants infested with rust can be treated, if you wish, with a sulphur-based spray at the first signs of trouble.

Basal rot

This is a fungus that affects any plants growing from bulbs, which in the allotment means garlic and onions and flowers such as daffodils. As a result, leaves yellow and die back and bulbs may rot. If garlic is affected its keeping qualities may be impaired, and even if it is dried out thoroughly it may not last the winter.

Foot rot

This serious fungal disease attacks the bases of stems of tomatoes, peas and beans. It is usually fatal. Once it is established it is unlikely that you will be able to save your plants. If it is a problem around your plot, use a fungicide as a preventative when plants are young. Since spores stay in the soil, crop rotation is also essential.

White rot

The symptoms of white rot, which can affect all members of the onion family, are very similar to those of basal rot, but it attacks more quickly and, in the case of garlic, is more likely to kill the plant outright. If you catch the problem early, you may be able to remove the most badly affected areas from garlic heads and save some of the cloves, but you need to take precautions to prevent future attacks. Cool, wet summers pose most risk. Onions and garlic with white rot are unlikely to keep well. Avoid planting onions or their relatives in an affected spot for as long as you can – which of course is easier on a larger plot.

It was definitely white rot, and a shock to see when we lifted what seemed to be really good-sized onions. However, we rubbed off and set aside all the affected outer layers before we left the crop out to dry and ripen off in the sun. For the winter we hung the best of them in string bags in the garage. We still managed to eat our own until well after Christmas. (Ruth)

Scab

Scabby brown blotches on potatoes, but also on fruit such as apples and pears, can spoil the looks of allotment crops. Unless scabs are deep enough to split the fruit or tuber flesh they are unlikely to affect keeping qualities, but it is wise to eat these before your perfect specimens. For potatoes, look for scab-resistant varieties. On fruit, use a fungicide at regular intervals from the appearance of the first flower buds until small fruit are well formed in early to mid summer.

White blister

This fungal disease of brassicas, fortunately rarely fatal, is a nuisance. On leaves and stems white blisters appear. The best treatment is just to remove any affected leaves as soon as you spot the problem. If stems are badly affected you may need to pull up and destroy whole plants.

Blight

Diseases called blight are the greatest scourge of tomatoes and potatoes. These are dealt with under their specific entries.

Fusarium wilt

This fungus is most likely to do damage to your allotment asters and sweet peas. Although well watered, plants wilt nonetheless. Stem bases turn black and plants are killed. Dusting roots of young plants with sulphur before they are set in their final positions is a good deterrent. Otherwise there is little you can do apart from keeping plants well fed and getting rid of diseased plants safely.

VIRUSES

Relatively few viral infections afflict allotment crops – the most usual is the leaf mosaic virus which makes affected leaves turn yellow and stunts plants, leading to poor, substandard harvests. Because they are spread by aphids – though also on tools and on gardeners' hands – the best prevention is to keep aphids at bay (see p. 93). There is no treatment for the virus itself. Good general hygiene is also vital.

Cucumber mosaic virus
This affects not only cucumbers but also their close relatives – marrows, squashes and courgettes. Prevention is as for leaf mosaic virus.

GREENHOUSES

Even without the heating only possible with electricity to hand, an allotment greenhouse has lots of advantages, whether for raising seeds and young plants or for growing cucumbers, tomatoes and more exotic, tender fruit and vegetables like melons, peppers and aubergines. Of course, you need a big enough plot to make space for a greenhouse, a sunny position away from trees, where the wind will not blow out the panes every week in winter, and a plot that is vandal free. Most of all, though, you need to be able to get to your greenhouse to water your produce regularly, or you will end up with a shrivelled mess.

> *A greenhouse on a plot, unless you're there every other day, is just going to get cremated out. I got a greenhouse for nothing from a house [in a nearby street] from people who didn't want it any more. A few of us went to collect it then put it up on my plot. (Jim Greenhill)*

Unless you are prepared to make a brick or concrete base for a wooden structure, the easiest choice for an allotment is one with an aluminium or rigid PVC frame which can be placed direct onto the ground (which needs clearing well first). Ideally you will need to be able to open the panes on the top of the house though you may be able to get enough ventilation in summer by propping the door open. Putting up the greenhouse is definitely a job for a calm day and for two or more people.

Inside the greenhouse, some kind of wooden staging will give you room for additional pots. Otherwise you can grow plants direct into the soil or in containers, as you prefer. One advantage of pots, though, is that you can add water-retaining granules to help conserve moisture.

> *The big secret to greenhouse cultivation seemed to be the soil – it needed lots of manure or compost every year as otherwise it became impoverished very quickly. (Alexa Stace)*

Tomatoes are by far the favourite greenhouse crop, and generally successful.

> *Tomatoes were the great success in the greenhouse: even in a warm summer the wind was always a problem for tomatoes grown outdoors, retarding their growth, and slowing down the ripening. I also had some success with peppers and aubergines, though they never grew as large as the ones in Tesco! Big disaster was cucumbers, which in theory can be grown with great success, but mine were always titchy and rather bitter. (Alexa Stace)*

Temperature and air control

Even in a poor summer a greenhouse is going to get too hot, so keen allotmenters fit temperature-controlled roof ventilators to their roof windows. They also wash the outside of the glass in late spring (but depending on the season) with a mixture of 1 part white emulsion to 100 parts of water. An alternative is to fit roller blinds, though they can be hard to keep clean. To keep the greenhouse as warm as possible in winter it may also be possible to rig up 'double glazing' using sheets of polythene or bubble wrap. The most superior greenhouses are, of course, double glazed.

In summer you need to be able to let pollinators fly freely, too:

> *The bees go in and out so the tomatoes are fine. (Sue Bryant)*

Watering

Apart from persuading allotment neighbours to help you out in your absence, capillary matting under pots and trays also works well, though is best for small pots. For a price you can get more sophisticated battery-operated irrigation systems, too.

I've seen lots of ways in which greenhouses are kept watered. One ingenious set-up has rainwater running into a butt from a narrow drain on the greenhouse roof. The butt is connected by a pipe with a tap into a capillary watering system so that plants are kept nicely damp for days on end. It even works well enough for the plot holder to go on holidays, though he still asks his neighbours to keep an eye on things. (Ruth)

Greenhouse health

If you whack your tomatoes in there you can control the blight. (Sue Bryant)

Greenhouse plants are most likely to suffer from fungal diseases and from pests such as whitefly and red spider mite. Fungi flourish in warm, wet conditions, so good ventilation is vital to their prevention, as is avoiding overwatering (always tempting if you're not at your plot every day). Sticky yellow traps hung in the greenhouse will attract and stop whitefly dead in their tracks, or you can try some of the biological controls on the market.

At the end of the season, on a sunny autumn day, you need to clean the greenhouse well. Unless you live almost next door it's probably going to be impossible to clean the glass with hot water, but a disinfectant in cold water should work well. Pots and trays can be taken home for a more rigorous sterilizing treatment.

BONFIRES AND ALLOTMENT RUBBISH

Allotment bonfires are good fun and serve the useful purpose of exterminating the agent of disease, but they are no longer considered eco-friendly and on many allotment sites are totally banned. So check out the rules rather than getting into trouble.

There's a real pleasure in playing with a bonfire, fiddling around with it to keep

*it alight and coming home from the allotment with your clothes, hair and skin
imbued with the smell of bonfire smoke after a couple of hours. (Ruth)*

Before you light up your piles of old Brussels sprout stems, raspberry canes and other
woody rubbish, check the rules of your site. If bonfires are allowed, but only if they are
guaranteed not to disturb people living nearby, then you may need to check the strength
and direction of the wind. A windy day is great for keeping the fire alight, but will
guarantee smoke billowing far and wide.

*We're allowed bonfires on weekdays only – and from about 3 or 4 o'clock
onwards. You have to make sure it's out before you go, and try to burn everything
as fast as possible. (Sue Bryant)*

When you are having a bonfire it is tempting just to bung some paper under your pile
and hope that it lights. This may work, but the Boy Scouts' method of beginning with a
wigwam of dry twigs (with paper if you wish) and adding to it works much better.

*Try starting with the driest material first to get a good blaze going before adding
the damper stuff. The added advantage of this is that a really hot fire will give
off much less smoke. If you have a piece of corrugated iron on the plot, fold it
over and use it as a funnel to draw air into the fire. It's a lot more effective than
lying down on the ground and blowing, though the latter could be considered an
essential part of the bonfire ritual. (Ruth)*

A metal incinerator is useful for keeping a bonfire confined but the same rules apply. If
not well ventilated it can produce even more smoke than a regular fire. It also gets very,
very hot, and should only be handled with thick gloves.

Unless the bonfire has reduced itself to a smoulder, put it out with a bucket of water
before you leave the plot – or ask a neighbour to keep an eye on it. When the fire is
finished, scatter the ashes around your raspberries or tomatoes, which will appreciate
them most.

Wood ash contains some nutrients but you can't rely on it solely. (Andrew Malleson)

Rubbish solutions

Even if bonfires are allowed on your site you are bound to have rubbish to dispose of. Save the big plastic bags that potting compost comes in and use them for separate types of rubbish: non-compostable weeds (e.g. convolvulus and horsetails), woody material and plastic and non-biodegradable materials. You may need an additional one for diseased plant material.

Skip days are great. Our council provides occasional skips for garden rubbish, so we save what we can and put it in the skip when it arrives. At Highgate we had to be vigilant to ward off non-allotmenters dumping furniture, old fridges and the like. (Ruth)

Otherwise – or if skip appearances are few and far between – you will have to take the bags to your local recycling centre. When you do, check where to put the contents of each one, and say exactly what's in it.

KEEPING RECORDS

If only for the fun of looking back at what you've grown, as well as your successes and failures, it is well worth keeping an allotment diary – if you have any energy left after all the cultivating, harvesting and preserving. Make a note of the weather and temperature when you make your records. Add notes about compost and fertilizer and any problems with pests and diseases.

I write a gardening diary and try to keep that going. You get so much encouragement. (Marta Scott)

As well as recording what you grew where, and how it did, keep a note of seed and plant varieties and any good or bad points, such as onion sets delivered with mould growing, or substandard – or high-quality – fruit bushes.

CHAPTER 3

GROWING VEGETABLES

From everyday crops like potatoes, runner beans and carrots, to more exotic vegetables such as fennel, pak choi and sweet potatoes, almost any vegetables can be grown at the allotment. The better tended and prepared your soil, and the more meticulous you are about weeding, the better your vegetables will be. All vegetables have their own particular likes and dislikes, and are grouped here in broad botanical groups, so combining plants that share similar horticultural needs.

It's nice to plan in the winter for what seeds you want to buy next season. (Pat Bence)

BEANS AND PEAS

Bean sticks are the epitome of the allotment landscape, and there are few vegetables to beat the allotment bean – whether runner or French, dwarf or climbing. Peas, too, are excellent on the plot. The trickiest part of cultivating these vegetables is getting good germination and protecting young plants from slugs, snails, rabbits and other pests (see pp. 86 – 95).

Before we put up rabbit-proof fencing we planted out runner beans three times – the third time swathed in netting – until we salvaged any worthwhile plants. (Ruth)

Broad beans

Broad beans are one of the most rewarding allotment crops. For early beans, seeds can be sown in October or November and overwintered, though you need a variety specifically bred for the purpose such as 'Aquadulce Claudia'. In spring, February (if it is warm enough), March and April are sowing months for allotment broad bean crops. 'Giant Exhibition Longpod' and 'Jubilee Hysor' are both great croppers.

Overwintering is by no means foolproof. If the season is cold you may get patchy results and plants that are a bit straggly from being decimated by the wind, but it is a good way of saving space for the many spring and summer crops, and of warding off disease.

I always sow broad beans overwintered because they're ready in May before the blackfly. (Chris Luck)

Well-manured ground is best for broad beans, with seeds planted at 15 cm (6 in) apart and about 5 cm (2 in) deep in double rows about 23 cm (9 in) wide. Even if the soil is warm and dry enough to plant seeds direct, they will benefit from the protection of a fleece until they germinate, and this will also help keep mice away. In colder places, or when spring weather is very cold and damp, they can be germinated in pots, cells or a deep seed tray.

I'd buy in the market half a pint of beans every few weeks to keep them going. (Pat Bence)

Broad beans don't need much attention, but if your plot is exposed to wind they will benefit from good supports. A neat way of doing this is to push in sticks at about four-plant intervals, attach string to the end stick, then weave the string between the plants. As the beans increase in height you can add another row or two of string above the first.

Blackfly are usually the only serious pests of broad beans. Pinching the tops out of the plants will help, and will also give you bigger pods. Do this as soon as you see signs of infestation.

We arrived at the allotment one June day to find a crop of broad beans that had looked perfect a couple of days before with many of the lower pods bitten open and the beans gone. It soon dawned that the squirrels we often saw in the trees in neighbouring gardens were the culprits. We hastily used sticks and netting to construct a 'gulag' around the plants; this averted any further trouble, and we did the same – but earlier in the season – in subsequent years to be on the safe side. (Ruth)

Late plantings of broad beans are especially susceptible – and even more so in wet summers – to chocolate spot, a fungal disease whose symptoms are perfectly described by its name. Once this strikes, the likelihood of getting a crop is virtually nil, so they are best pulled up.

I never have faith in late broad beans. (Donald Binney)

French beans

There are two ways of growing French beans – either as dwarf crops or as climbers. There are lots of sorts to choose from, including flat and rounded pods, beans coloured in purple or yellow, and those like the haricot best harvested for drying.

Being shallow-rooted, French beans appreciate a position that is as sheltered as possible; this is not always easy to supply on an exposed site. They are also vulnerable to frost, which means that you need to plan your sowing and provide protection if necessary.

French beans will germinate if planted directly into the ground, but my experience is that the irregularities of the weather, especially early in the season, leads to many 'blind' germinations of plants with no leaves. It's much more reliable to sow them in pots or cells and to germinate them indoors or in a greenhouse or frame. (Ruth)

For a really early crop, sowing can begin in April; young plants can then be set out under fleece, cloches or polythene until the risk of frost has passed. To help provide the moisture they like it helps to earth up the soil around dwarf bean plants a little as they are becoming established. Slugs and snails will go straight for your young bean plants if they are not protected, as will rabbits. The newest fast-germinating varieties are bred to produce late-season crops.

This is a selection of good French bean varieties.

'Deliniel'	Dwarf. Round green pods
'The Prince'	Dwarf. Flat green pods
'Valdor'	Dwarf. Round yellow pods
'Pongo'	Dwarf. Autumn cropper; sow July–August
'Safari'	Dwarf, Kenya type. Slender green pods
'Blue Lake'	Climber. Round green pods
'Algarve'	Climber. Large flat green pods
'Empress'	Climber. Round purple pods
'Borlotto Fretongue'	Climber. Italian borlotti bean for drying

Runner beans

Although commonly known as 'scarlet runners' from their flower colour, modern varieties such as 'Désirée' are actually white flowered. If you don't want to put up sticks there are good dwarf varieties like 'Pickwick' and 'Hestia' (which has red and white blooms) to choose from. If tenderness is your goal, then select a stringless bean like 'Polestar' or 'Butler'; if your aim is to win the 'longest bean' class in your annual vegetable show, then grow 'Enorma'. You can also select varieties for early cropping.

Runner beans are deep rooted and need good, well-manured soil. Preparation for your runner beans can begin in autumn by digging the 46-cm (18-in) wide trench where you will grow them. If you make it a good 23 cm (9 in) deep you can throw in all kinds of leafy, compostable material from the end of the summer crops and leave it to rot over the winter. Alternatively, dig a slightly shallower trench in spring, about a month to six weeks before you aim to plant your seedlings, and add a good layer of well-rotted manure.

In the winter I dug my trench ready for beans and filled it with all my compost, eggshells and whatever. (Pat Bence)

When you are ready to set either seeds or plants, replace the topsoil in the middle of the trench, leaving two straight furrows. The sticks then go on the outside edge, pushed well into the ground to avoid plant roots and to keep them stable in the wind. The sticks for the beans (both runners and climbing French) can go in before or after planting.

We like to put bean sticks in later, once plants are growing well. For years we tied the canes, with horizontal canes slotted into the Vs, but now we use plastic clips which are quicker to fix and much more secure. Except for the strongest gales that sweep in from the Dorset coast, they seem to be able to withstand high winds. For those tightly tied thick string is needed as well. This year they have nearly collapsed and we've had to put string right around and fix it to the posts along the allotment sides. (Ruth)

If you don't manage to get around to trenching, don't worry. Just dig two good furrows and add manure – either fresh, well rotted or the concentrated kind – before planting. Equally, if you want to grow just a few beans up a wigwam, set your plants into generous individual holes, again with plenty of compost. An alternative to sticks is to grow runner beans up sheets of wide plastic or wire mesh which you can roll up in autumn and reuse. It needs to be firmly attached to strong posts placed at intervals of a few feet.

As with French beans, you can plant runner bean seeds direct into the ground, but starting them in cells or pots is much more reliable. Don't plant them out until the risk of frosts is over.

Runners (and dwarf beans) like foliage feeding when you first put them in. After about a week do a foliar feed with a fine rose on your watering can, then about a week later do it again. (Mike Wiffen)

Take steps to keep off slugs and other usual pests, and water beans well throughout their growing season. Be careful not to swamp them. If you overwater them you will encourage the roots to flourish near the soil surface rather than penetrate deep into the soil.

They're a subtropical crop first brought in for their flowers so they need water and heat. Don't put cold water on them at night (which is difficult if you're working). Do it at midday when the sun's at its height. That sends the vapour up and sets your flowers. (Mike Wiffen)

Some allotment gardeners take special pains to keep their runner beans watered:

In the winter open up your bean trench and measure the length to within 6 inches of each end. Purchase a length of drainpipe the width you measured plus 6 feet, plus two right-angle joints. Dig a deep trench and fill it with kitchen waste during the winter, then prior to planting lay a thick layer of newspaper in the trench. Take the piece of drainpipe that is going to go across the plot and drill small holes through it along its entire length. Lay it on the newspaper and fix the right-angled joints, pointing upwards, one at each end. Cut the 6-foot length of pipe in half and slot into the right-angled joints, pointing upwards. Put a level on the pipe and adjust it with stones placed underneath. Cover the newspaper over the top of the pipe, secure and fill in the rest of the trench with topsoil. You now have an underground watering system which delivers water to where it is needed, the root system. The newspaper will stop the holes clogging up, the 3 feet of pipe each end means you don't have to bend to water and you can water from each end of the row. (Tim Callard)

Some pests are particularly partial to a runner bean:

We lost a lot of runner beans and slugs and snails ate all the young plants. The ones from the second sowing slowly crept up the poles then, hey presto, we were picking three bags of beans a day. (Ken Daniels)

Runner beans will appreciate some extra feed – either as liquid or a top dressing – once the pods begin to set. To prevent them getting over-straggly, pinch out the tops once they reach the tops of the poles – you may need to take stepladders or telescopic loppers to the allotment to do this.

Wind can decimate runner beans by blowing all the blossom off before beans have a chance to be fertilized. Another way of ensuring good fertilization is to choose them some good companions:

I always plant my dahlias next to my runner beans because of the bees. The one year I didn't do it I had hardly any beans. I came back to it this year and I had loads. They seem to protect each other. (Maureen Nightingale)

Peas

Eaten straight from the pod, fresh peas are a vegetable from heaven. So good that once your children discover them you'll find your crop ravaged by human 'pests'. The first, crisp mangetouts of the season do not quite match up, but are still delicious. You can also grow tiny petits pois or old-fashioned marrowfat peas which can be eaten fresh or dried to use in soups and casseroles.

To get enough 'regular' peas to be worthwhile you need several rows. Because of the pressure on space of summer and autumn crops, and to have peas early in the season, it pays to get your first sowings of peas in during February – or even overwinter them with the protection of fleece, polythene or cloches. They like a well-composted soil with good drainage, especially if they are to survive periods of cold and damp. Ideally, aim to grow fairly small amounts in succession. You will also need to plan suitable supports, depending on the height of the mature plants.

Peas are best sown in drills about 10 cm (4 in) deep and wide enough to accommodate three rows placed in zigzags with about 5 cm (2 in) between each. Allow 60 cm (2 ft) between parallel drills. If you are planting in the autumn, sow seeds a little more thickly as you are bound to have some casualties; you can always thin them out later. To prevent seeds being eaten by mice, soak them in paraffin overnight before you plant them (the odour is a rodent deterrent). You can also try edging the row with twigs of holly or gorse. Easiest of all is to cover the row with fleece, pegged down firmly:

As well as pegging netting over an early planting of mangetouts, we thought we had made sure there were no entry points by putting a line of stones along the edge to make it secure. But no luck. A mouse still managed to eat its way along the whole row. The next sowing we covered in fleece, which did the trick. Better yet were sowings made in cells and planted out later. (Ruth)

Once seeds germinate, they will need little thinning except to avoid overcrowding. Be sure they do not get too wet as they can be susceptible to damping off. When they are about 10 cm (4 in) high they will need supporting – left to droop they will be even more vulnerable to slugs and snails. Rather than smooth sticks, they need supports that will allow them to cling on by their many tendrils. You can use criss-crossed twigs, lines of string or wire attached at 7.5 to 10 cm (3 to 4 in) intervals between bamboo canes set about 30 cm (1 ft) apart, or two pieces of netting supported vertically on bamboo poles, making a perimeter around the plants. If you live in the country you may be able to buy traditionally made pea sticks, which will last for many years. Otherwise, try improvising. Prunings from garden shrubs and trees, cut canes from autumn raspberries and any sticks you can garner from the allotment boundary can all be pressed into use.

> *Being short of pea sticks one year we took a walk around the allotments and in a far corner discovered a pile of tree prunings from one of the gardens backing onto the plot. We fell on them gladly and they lasted us two years. Now we mostly use canes from autumn raspberries. (Ruth)*

Strong plants will need little attention apart from watering. A good mulch put on after a thorough soaking will help keep peas moist. The advantage of early sowings is that they are less likely to be attacked by the pea moth, whose caterpillars hatch inside the pods and consume the contents. Growing garlic near your peas can help deter the adult moths, or you can use an organic garlic spray on the flowers. If you see signs of silver mottling of the leaves and pods, caused by pea thrips, the same spray will also be effective, or you can use another form of insecticide, following instructions carefully.

The following are good pea choices.

'Kelvedon Wonder'	Early, good for sowing in succession. Height 45 cm (18 in)
'Feltham First'	Can be overwintered. Makes strong plants. Height 45 cm (18 in)
'Early Onward'	Heavy cropper, quick maturing. Height 75 cm (30 in)
'Greensage'	Sweet peas, heavy cropping. Height 75 cm (30 in)
'Oregon Sugar Pod'	Mangetout, can be overwintered. Height 90 cm (3 ft)
'Delikata'	Can be used as a mangetout or, if pods are left to mature, as a shelled pea. Height 75 cm (30 in)
'PeaWee'	Petits pois. Height 45 cm (18 in)
'Maro'	Marrowfat pea.

BRASSICAS

Whether you are growing cabbage or kale, Brussels sprouts or broccoli, there are certain conditions that all members of the cabbage family need. First and foremost they need fertile soil that has been manured in advance of planting – ideally in the autumn before. They are also fussy about soil acidity, liking a slightly alkaline environment around pH 7.2 (which will also help to deter club root), so you will need to lime the soil in late winter or early spring if necessary. Brassicas like their roots to be firm; if they are blown about on a windy site 'root rock' will hinder their growth. One good way to ensure that roots are firm is to avoid loosening the soil in spring. You can tread it down if the weather is not too wet.

My plot's not good for cauliflowers – the soil's too loose here. (Doug Chainey)

All brassicas are thirsty and hungry, needing plenty of water and regular feeding if they are to thrive. Especially when young, they are a magnet for pigeons, slugs and cabbage white caterpillars – and rabbits – so need protection against all of these. You also need to look out for attacks from flea beetles, aphids and whitefly. Downy mildew can also be a problem, so choose seed bred for resistance to this fungus. Cabbage root fly is a pest of all brassicas from which plants will need protection.

We had spent an afternoon absorbed in planting out brassicas. When we returned the following weekend we were shocked to see the whole patch decimated by pigeons. We netted them and they recovered eventually, but every brassica planted out ever since has been immediately swathed in netting – just in case. (Ruth)

Many brassicas are best started off in an allotment seedbed or in pots or trays at home. They don't like to be crowded so make the effort to sow them thinly or, if you prefer, sow them two or three seeds to a pot or cell. After germination, seedlings will mature more quickly with some protection – either a cold frame or greenhouse if in trays, or fleece or polythene on the plot. Once large enough to handle they need to be thinned to about 5 cm (2 in) or potted on into individual pots. The exceptions are vegetables such as pak choi and Chinese cabbage which dislike being transplanted.

When planting out brassicas, choose a cool day – too much heat will make them wilt horribly. Make a hole with a dibber or a slender trowel and pour in some water from a can. Set the plant in the hole and firm up the soil all around it with your hands. If you're careful you can also use your heel to make the earth extra firm. Water them in generously.

Cabbage

With good planning you can pick allotment cabbage almost all the year round, though in summer you may prefer to give the space to other vegetables. Of all the brassicas, cabbages are among the easiest to grow, but they will still need firm ground that has been well manured, regular feeding and plenty of water through the growing season.

Ammonia is good for cabbages. It's what you put underneath them that counts – I put manure. (Mike Wiffen)

For summer cabbages, including Savoy and red cabbage, start sowing seed in March; for all kinds of autumn cabbages get seeds going in April and May. Spring cabbages need to be sown in mid to late summer and left to stand over the winter. Ideally you want plants that are strong enough by mid October to survive the winter cold but not so overfed that they mature too quickly. If planted too late they will be vulnerable to pests, diseases and the winter weather.

If you plant them too early spring cabbages always bolt if it stays warm through the autumn. (Ruth)

Once cabbage seedlings have four or five good leaves they can be set in their permanent positions, about 45 to 60 cm (18 in to 2 ft) apart in all directions. Discard any that don't have good root systems and plant as deeply as possible. Firm them in well and protect them from birds and other predators.

Spring cabbages need some extra treatment. In November, earth up around the plants, making a continuous low ridge. This helps to drain surplus water away from the stalks and stabilizes plants against winter winds. In a cold winter, fleece or cloches will give added protection until the weather warms up.

These are some popular cabbage choices that should do well.

Summer

'Greyhound'	Early maturing; pointed heads
'Puma'	Round, solid heads; stands well
'Mila'	Round; Savoy type
'Derby Day'	Early; round heads; bolt resistant

Late summer/autumn

'Kilaxy'	Round; good club root resistance
'Picador'	Round, firm heads
'Minicole'	Small, round, bright green heads
'Ruby Perfection'	Red cabbage; small heads

Early/late winter

'Holland Winter White'	White cabbage for coleslaw; cut and keep in November
'Tundra'	Frost hardy; round heads; will stand all winter
'January King 3'	Round heads; will last all winter

Spring

'Durham Elf'	Pointed, dark green leaves
'Mastergreen'	Hardy; can be planted in early July for autumn cropping
'Pixie'	Very early; small pointed heads

Kale

It's a nice vegetable – I just do the seeds in the greenhouse and prick them out. (Mike Wiffen)

The hardiest of all the brassicas, kale is a great winter stand-by, best eaten when the leaves are small and tender. As well as the traditional curly kale, like 'Dwarf Green Curled', you can also grow 'Redbor' or another of the new red varieties, or a variety of cavolo negro such as 'Nero di Toscana Precole', an Italian kale with slimmer, smoother, dark purplish-green leaves.

Kale seeds, planted in April or May, need plenty of space throughout their growing period if they are to form large, healthy plants. By July they will be ready to plant permanently and will need a good 60 cm (2 ft) between plants in all directions. Although less fussy than some brassicas, they need to be firmly set in the ground and, through the winter, firmed in with your foot every now and again. If they seem to be floppy, support them with canes.

Brussels sprouts

Sprouts can be tricky to grow, and take up a lot of space, but are well worth the effort if they are a vegetable you like. Most of all they like firm soil – root rock will hinder their growth – as well as lots of food and water.

> *By the middle of a windy Dorset winter, some of our sprouts were loose and 'blown'. Our neighbour – a superb gardener – came up with a great tip. 'Over next winter,' he said, 'when it's not too wet, keep treading on the ground you're going to use for them next year. By the time you come to plant it will be nice and hard. And don't forget,' he added, 'sprouts are greedy feeders.' (Ruth)*

Luckily for vegetable gardeners the latest F1 sprout varieties are much more reliable than in the past. You can also choose good early-maturing types such as 'Cromwell' and 'Brilliant' which are ready in September, but vulnerable to frost. For later-maturing, longer-standing, more frost-resistant sprouts choose varieties such as 'Montgomery', 'Clodius' or 'Bedford Winter Harvest'. The latest and most frost tolerant sorts of all include 'Wellington'. For sprouts with a difference try the striking purple 'Red Bull'.

Raise sprouts like other brassicas, sowing seed in late March or early April and planting them out about 60 cm (2 ft) apart. If you put them any closer they will grow small and spindly. Reject any plants without good roots or strong growing points. In a windy plot it helps to stake plants individually, tying them firmly to keep the roots as stable as possible. As they mature or die off, remove the lower leaves to let in light and air.

Sprouting broccoli and calabrese

Dubbed 'poor man's asparagus', sprouting broccoli is an excellent 'cut and come again' stand-by for spring. As well as the traditional purple it also comes in a white variety. Calabrese makes larger green central heads but after these have been cut and eaten will usually grow more smaller 'side heads'. Both are grown in a similar way, though their cropping times vary, and there are enough varieties available to give you a harvest from late spring right through to the autumn. The chart below suggests some good choices for a long harvesting season.

Begin the sowing season in March with calabrese seeds, which are generally quicker maturing than sprouting broccoli, which will follow in April. Calabrese can be planted in succession through May, depending on variety and maturing time. When planting out, you can space calabrese at about 50 cm (20 in) apart in all directions, but sprouting broccoli need a generous 60 cm (2 ft) minimum. Follow all the general brassica guidelines and stake tall plants if they are likely to be affected by wind.

Early spring

'Early Purple Sprouting Blend' Mix of seeds gives plants that mature in succession from late January or February to April

'White Sprouting' Hardy; crops February or March to April

Late spring

'Kabuki' Calabrese; quick maturing

'Nabana' Calabrese with crinkled Savoy-style leaves

Summer/autumn

'Bordeaux' Purple sprouting; crops July to October

'Autumn Spear' Calabrese; crops September–November

'Romanesco Celio' Italian type, pale green head; crops July–September

Autumn/winter

'Samson F1' Calabrese; mildew resistant

'Garnet' Purple sprouting; harvest from December

Choosing the seed mixture that gives purple sprouting plants that mature at different times really pays off. We have grown the white sprouting, but it doesn't have quite the good flavour of the purple. (Ruth)

Chinese broccoli

For something totally different, with the benefit of being really quick to mature, plant some seeds of Chinese broccoli (Chinese kale). Although the young leaves and buds are also eaten, this oriental vegetable is grown for its thick, succulent stems which are delicious when cooked. The top few inches of the flowering stalks are picked as soon as the flowers appear, which can be as little as a couple of months after sowing. The seed can be sown, either direct or in a seedbed, from early spring to late autumn, then transplanted or thinned to 20 to 25 cm (8 to 10 in) apart.

Cauliflowers

They are the hungriest crop of all. (Maureen Nightingale)

The trickiest of all the brassicas, good cauliflowers are the signatures of allotment 'professionals'. They are particularly intolerant of any form of stress, such as drying out, which will reduce head growth, a phenomenon known as 'buttoning'. They are also prey to whitefly and caterpillars.

Like other brassicas, cauliflowers are bred in varieties that mature in different seasons and, technically, winter cauliflowers are a form of broccoli. Cauliflowers need very well-prepared soil, which must always be alkaline, and lots of food and water. As with other brassicas, root rock will seriously slow their growth.

For the allotment cauliflower novice, a good way to start is to plant seeds of a reliable variety like 'All the Year Round' in March or April, to mature in mid to late summer or early autumn; or in May, to mature in October and November. If you use a seedbed on the plot make sure you add some extra peat to the soil and sow the seed sparingly, thinning seedlings to 10 cm (4 in) apart as soon as they are big enough to handle. If you plant them in trays, pot them on.

When they have five or six leaves your plants are ready for permanent planting. Put summer cauliflowers about 60 cm (2 ft) apart in all directions, putting plenty of water in each hole and firming the soil well.

I did plant them well apart – it definitely makes a difference. (Maureen Nightingale)

A top dressing of compost or a liquid feed is helpful at this stage. Add anti cabbage fly collars if you wish until plants are a good size. If the weather turns cold and dry after you have set out your plants, cover them with some fleece or a cloche to help keep them at a constant temperature.

All you need to do now – though this is not easy in dry summers – is to tend them carefully so that they are never short of water, and feed them regularly through the growing season. An additional mulch of compost put on after heavy rain, or a very thorough watering, can help to keep the roots moist later in the season. As the heads – the curds – begin to mature, fold the outer leaves over them to prevent them becoming discoloured or damaged.

You also need to keep off whitefly and caterpillars through the growing season:

They were yellow, stinking things. When we picked them whitefly flew out and there were things crawling inside them like nits. Washing them didn't even help. We gave up after a year. It just wasn't worth it. (Ken Daniels)

Cauliflowers for different seasons need different timings. For cropping in late spring and early summer, sow a variety such as 'Mayflower F1' under cloches in October, thin them out and keep them protected through the winter before planting out in April. Or sow in a propagator or heated greenhouse in February. Be sure to harden the plants off well before you plant them out.

For cropping in early spring sow seed such as 'Galleon' or 'Walcheren Winter 3*' in an allotment seedbed in late May, and transplant in July.

One common reason why cauliflowers fail is a lack of boron. Even if your soil is already alkaline, try mixing 30 g (1 oz) of borax with half a bucket of sharp sand for spreading on an area of 1 square metre (1 square yard).

LEAFY CROPS

All leafy vegetables share a need for plenty of water to prevent them shooting quickly to seed. Swiss chard has the bonus of having edible stems as well as leaves, though they can be bitter and not to everyone's taste. It is well worth experimenting with some of the newer oriental leaf crops to see which you like, and which will flourish on your plot. Slugs and snails attack leafy vegetables, as do rabbits and pigeons. You also need to look out for aphids of all kinds. The thinnings of all these vegetables can be eaten raw or cooked. Premature yellowing of the leaves is a sign that plants are short of nutrients.

Spinach

Though quite greedy of space, spinach is a reliable vegetable, whether you choose the quick-growing summer type preferred by purist cooks, or one of the perpetual varieties. Spinach will appreciate some shade if you can supply it. In any event, be prepared for plenty of watering in dry spells.

A variety of summer spinach like 'Triathlon' or 'Scenic' will germinate in a matter of days and be ready to pick in a few weeks, so you can sow it between other vegetables such as potatoes. Try to keep your enthusiasm under control and plant little and often. Early crops, sown from late February or early March, are most useful as they are ready well before you are supplied with summer staples like beans and peas, as are late ones.

> We always put in a last sowing of spinach in August. As well as giving us a late crop after most summer veg are over it will, if the weather is mild, survive through to spring and sprout again. This year we were still picking it in June. (Ruth)

Summer spinach needs plenty of water to stop it from running too quickly to seed and water retention will be helped by digging in plenty of compost. Varieties such as 'Cezanne' and 'Rhino' are marketed as being resistant to both bolting and downy mildew.

> A crop for free: some summer spinach was left and allowed to go to seed in an allotment corner. The winter was mild and in February we discovered a mass of seedlings. Dug up, separated, transplanted and fed, by late March they had produced an abundance of leaves. (Ruth)

Perpetual spinach, also known as spinach beet and New Zealand spinach, needs a more permanent position and is best sown in April and again in July. Despite its name it is in fact a biennial and will seed in its second year, so in effect needs raising annually. As with summer spinach, rows placed 60–90 cm (2–3 ft) apart are best thinned to leave about 20 cm (8 in) between plants. Longer-lived crops will need general, regular feeding.

Swiss chard

Often sold as 'leaf beet', Swiss chard is grown like spinach but it is hardier – and both stems and leaves are tasty. Chard looks lovely in the allotment too, whether you grow the white-stemmed sort (confusingly, also called sea kale), one of the red-stemmed (rainbow) rhubarb chards or a yellow-stemmed variety such as 'Bright Yellow'. Rainbow chard has multicoloured stems in white, pink, red and yellow. Given well-manured ground and plenty of water, seeds sown in May will give you a crop by late summer while a second sowing in July provides a welcome crop the following April.

Chard thrives best if you thin it well, so space mature plants about 23 cm (9 in apart), and keep picking the leaves.

Pak choi, mizuna and oriental greens

Quick to mature, pak choi is a rewarding autumn vegetable for the allotment and a perfect stir-fry ingredient. In a crowded plot a good place for it is in the ground occupied by peas or broad beans after these have been harvested. Slugs love it.

Plant seeds in late summer, allowing about 40 cm (16 in) between rows. Put them where they will mature, since (as well as heat and drought) they hate being transplanted. They need thinning to about 20 cm (8 in). Being brassicas, they need protection, when young, from flea beetle. An early sowing, in March, under fleece, is a welcome gap-filler when there is not much else to pick.

The pak choi was maturing nicely, then the autumn turned very dry and warm. Before we knew it the crop had bolted into flower. The lower leaves were just about edible but there were no nice hearts. (Ruth)

Like pak choi, mizuna, also called Kyona or potherb mustard, is an oriental vegetable perfect for stir-fries. It also does best if planted in late summer or early spring, which will reduce its bolting tendencies. Look out, too, for mustards, some of which have pretty red foliage, and chop suey greens. Oriental mixtures, sold under names such as 'Spicy Green Mix', are quick and easy and in a warm season will mature in as little as four weeks.

I'm doing Oriental greens now [September]; later seems to suit them better. (Marta Scott)

EDIBLE STEMS

The two main allotment crops grown for their stems are asparagus and celery. Florence fennel is included here too since the edible parts are the swollen and clustered bases of the stems. Although each of these vegetables needs its own special care, give them all good soil and plenty of space.

Asparagus

An allotment asparagus bed will be very productive if you're lucky with the soil and avoid the dreaded beetle. To have enough asparagus to be worthwhile over its short cropping season you need at least a dozen plants, which will take up a significant amount of space. But the taste of fresh allotment asparagus is so divine that you may think it well worth it. Once established, a good asparagus bed needs relatively little attention and will last some 20 years.

It is worth planning for asparagus well in advance if you can. Choose a sunny spot, ideally sheltered from the wind, where there are as few perennial weeds as possible. If your soil is so light that water drains through it in a matter of hours, you may need to take a couple of years over this preparation or consider importing topsoil for a raised bed.

March and April are the traditional months for planting so, in the late summer and autumn of the year before, remove or kill off as many perennial weeds as possible and manure well. Heavy clay will benefit from being broken up by the addition of sharp sand. If you select one of the varieties now available for autumn planting, manure well in spring and leave the ground uncultivated – except for a few salads – in the months before planting.

Male asparagus plants are most convenient to grow as they do not spread seedlings around the plot. Unless you are ultra patient, and want to grow plants from seed, order one-year-old plants (crowns), possibly mixing varieties to extend your cropping season. 'Connover's Colossal', a heavy, mid-season cropper, is an all-time favourite, or you could try the early season 'Gijnlim F1' or even 'Purple Pacific' which is tender enough to eat raw.

Asparagus crowns need to be planted in trenches about 23 cm (9 in) deep and 30 cm (1 ft) wide, set 1 m (3 ft) apart. The base of the trench needs to be flat enough for you to be able to spread out the roots of the crowns about 45 cm (18 in) apart. Cover them with soil as quickly as you can to prevent them drying out. If you wish you can earth them up as the shoots emerge.

> *We had ordered our asparagus spears by mail, but awful weather and pressure of work meant that we were not as prepared as we might have been. The crowns arrived in the middle of the week, but it was impossible to plant them until the weekend. It was cold and rainy all day on Saturday so by Sunday afternoon we knew we would have to brave it. In a steady downpour we dug two trenches and more or less hurled the crowns into it. That was the best asparagus we have ever grown – thanks, probably, to superbly fertile soil near the Thames. (Ruth)*

When spears emerge, resist cutting them in the first year – and even in the second year, crop them only sparingly. This is essential to allow them to build up crown strength. Keep them well watered and give them a regular twice-yearly feed – a mulch of compost in the autumn and a lighter feed, such as a sprinkling of concentrated manure, in spring. Although the spears are unbelievably strong, be careful that they do not have to push up through lumps of unrotted manure. Every autumn, once the leaves and stems have turned yellow, and before composting, cut them down to about 2.5 cm (1 in). If you are allowed bonfires, they make a great blaze – and burning them also helps to control asparagus beetle.

Other routine jobs with asparagus are to keep them free of competition from weeds, especially perennial ones.

> *The trouble with asparagus is that it ends up smothered with couch grass and other perennial weeds. (Robin Barrett)*

You also need to keep an eagle eye open for asparagus beetles. The adults of these pests are a vivid reddish yellow and black, though their voracious, greyish larvae are harder to spot. They do not affect the spears, but feast on the leaves and bark of the mature shoots, killing them off and affecting the crowns. Apart from picking off beetles and their grubs and destroying them, the best remedy is a pyrethrum spray.

Celery

Celery comes in two types – self-blanching and trench celery – of which the former needs less attention and is easier to grow, though it is not frost hardy. To do well with either sort of celery you will need well-composted, well-manured soil. You will also need to be able to water your crop frequently. It generally needs a lot of work.

> *I tried celery once but it got eaten up by slugs – and you have to earth it up and wrap it in paper. The supermarkets have proved that they can produce a better stick of celery than I ever could. (Robin Barrett)*

Seeds of self-blanching celery, such as 'Loretta', 'Galaxy' and 'Golden Self-Blanching', and trench varieties such as 'Hopkins Fenlander', 'Giant Pascal' and the pink 'Giant Red' all need starting indoors at a temperature of 10–13ºC (50–55ºF) during March (you can make a later sowing in mid-April for a further crop). When seedlings are large enough to handle, prick them out into trays and, as the weather improves, harden them off. They should be ready to plant out by late May.

> *I get on better with self-blanching celery. It is good planted in a square – that keeps it much darker. (Doug Chainey)*

At this point, cultivation methods diverge. For self-blanching celery, simply transplant seedlings to the plot, placing them in a block with about 23 cm (9 in) between each. Water them well before you move them and, as you lift them from their tray, try to disturb the roots as little as possible. Water them in well and firm the soil. Keep them well watered and give them an occasional feed until they are ready to harvest in late summer.

For trench celery, the tradition is to grow a double row, with plants 23 cm (9 in) apart and with 45 cm (18 in) between rows, in a winter-dug trench 30 cm (1 ft) deep lined with well-rotted compost. Set your established plants in the trench and water them in well. In late summer, cut off any suckers from the base one and tie around each a double layer of newspaper or black polythene, securing the string firmly. Then use some of the soil from the ridges at the sides of the trench to cover plants to about halfway up their stems. Repeat this earthing up twice more (watering well each time), allowing three to four weeks between each earthing, so that by October just the leafy tops emerge from the top of a sloping ridge (as for earthed up potatoes). Dig them as you need them, though it may help to surround them with some straw if very cold, frost spells are predicted.

Both carrot and celery fly will attack young celery plants so you may need to protect them with fine mesh netting or fleece. As a precaution against boron deficiency, which makes celery stems cracked and brown, add borax to the soil before you plant. You only need a very little. A tablespoon is enough to treat 17 sq m (20 sq yards) and is best applied mixed with fine sand.

I wish I had known about borax when I first tried growing celery – and celery fly too. Though we did get some rather weedy stems of self-blanching celery the plants were never up to much. The fact that we couldn't get to water them most days in dry weather didn't help either. (Ruth)

Florence fennel

Once you have harvested all your winter cabbages and early spinach, use the space for a crop of Florence fennel. In any event you need to wait until the weather is warm before you begin seed planting. For big bulbs try a variety such as 'Goal' or 'Sirio' and sow seeds thinly where plants will mature (they dislike being disturbed by transplanting) in drills about 12 mm (½ in) deep and about 30 cm (1 ft) apart. As plants mature, gradually thin them to about 15 cm (6 in); if you are not growing fennel in the herb garden, the tops of the thinnings can be used in exactly the same way.

A wet but warm summer gave us a wonderful crop of fennel, with big bulbs standing right through until late November. The following baking hot, drought-ridden year, watering was a problem. Seeds germinated well but we did not thin them quickly enough and the plants shot almost straight to seed. (Ruth)

As the fennel bulbs start to form, keep the row well weeded and, as you weed, push soil up against them to keep them firm and white. Otherwise, apart from an occasional liquid feed or top dressing, they need little attention.

ROOT VEGETABLES

Vegetables that mature underground – which includes here potatoes as well as true root crops like carrots – mostly do well on allotments, though they tend to take up quite a lot of space. They need fertile, well-manured, water-retentive soil, but you need to avoid manuring the soil in the season before planting or you will end up with forked roots. Most like an alkaline soil, so add lime if necessary. Scattering a concentrated manure or chicken pellets works well for all root crops. Young plants need protecting from slugs and snails, rabbits and similar pests. Those that are brassicas (turnips, radishes, swedes) need protection from flea beetle and can be susceptible to club root.

Radishes

For me there can be few finer sensations than early radishes pulled up, washed under the allotment tap and eaten there and then.(Ruth)

Because they mature quickly – in about four weeks in the height of summer – the radish rule is to sow seed little and often.

With fleece or other protection, the first radishes of the year can be sown in late February or early March. Elongated 'French Breakfast' and round-rooted 'Scarlet Globe' are two traditional choices, or you can buy packets of mixed seeds for a variety of shapes and sizes. If you sow seed quite thickly you can thin out the crop as it matures, but above all you need to keep them well watered and free of flea beetle (see p. 95).

Large-rooted winter radishes in red (such as 'Mantanghong') or white (such as 'White Icicle' or 'April Cross') are a good crop to put in during June or July, once harvested crops like broad beans allow you some extra space. These need thinning to about 15 cm (6 in) apart and protecting from frost.

Beetroot

If you love beetroot there is nothing to better allotment-grown, whether it's thinnings the size of golf balls or soup made from the last overblown remnants of the crop. Equally, good uncooked beetroot is so hard to find in the shops. Of the round or globe varieties, 'Boltardy' is a justifiably reliable favourite but 'Globe 2' has a denser colour. Of the long-rooted varieties, 'Cylindrica' is a good choice. Or you can grow something more funky like 'Chioggia' with flesh ringed in red and white or the yellow variety like 'Burpee's Golden'. 'Blankoma White' is just that.

When sowing beetroot seed, remember that in most varieties (the exceptions are the 'monogram' varieties like 'Solo' or 'Modena') the seeds are actually clusters of three or four seeds fused together, so you need to space them well and be prepared for lots of thinning. Sowing can begin in mid March, if the soil is warm enough, and carry on until July to give you a succession of crops.

The fiddly business of thinning beetroot is one of my own allotment pleasures. Although they won't always take well, I can't usually resist the temptation of using thinned plants to fill in any gaps in the row. The textbooks say you shouldn't do this, but it can be worth a try. If they don't thrive then you haven't really lost anything. (Ruth)

Once seedlings are established, and a couple of true leaves have emerged, you can begin thinning – a job best done after it has rained – leaving the strongest seedling of each group in place. As the plants develop you can keep thinning until plants are about 10 cm (4 in) apart.

This is an old hint from Nottinghamshire miners. When beetroot get to the size of gob stoppers, go up and down the row with salt down the side – just ordinary salt. Only do it once, then water it in. It's a fertilizer. It's what farmers used on sugar beet. (Mike Wiffen)

You will need to keep beetroot watered in dry weather, but in good soil it is remarkably drought resistant and generally free of diseases. They can be left in the ground all winter, with some fleece to protect them, but beware of other problems:

I grow beetroot in a slight trench about 6 inches deep and sow it normally. As they grow I pull the soil over them and that keeps them red and fresh. It also keeps off the field mice. (Doug Chainey)

Carrots

There is just no comparison between home grown carrots and shop bought ones – even those sold as organic. But carrots can be tricky to grow. They are fussy about soil, and are plagued by the carrot fly, and even the newest varieties such as 'Maestro', 'Flyaway' and 'Resistafly' are not immune from infestation.

Before choosing from the seed catalogues, which offer every type of carrot from the classic long, pointed type to purple, yellow and bright red varieties, you need to decide how much space to allow and whether you want to grow carrots that will mature both early and late. The advantage of very early varieties like 'Primo' is that they can be ready before the flies attack. Alternatively, seed sown after 1 June is likely to miss the first, strong generation of these pests. Very late sown crops may avoid them altogether.

All need to be sown in shallow drills about 23 cm (9 in apart). Sowing carrot seed thinly enough to avoid overcrowding can be tricky:

I mix the seed with a handful of soil before I plant them. I have sometimes had to reseed some gaps but they always catch up. (Ruth)

Germination can also be mixed:

Carrots have been entirely unpredictable. I had one year when I put in two or three packets and nothing germinated. (Edward Probert)

Putting flowers next to carrots is said to help keep off carrot fly, but experience does not necessarily bear this out.

French marigolds keep carrot fly off – allegedly. But most of them were eaten completely. (Damien Grove)

I was told that the best way to keep off carrot fly is to hoe them every day. (Mary Osmond)

Or you can try making use of a taller crop:

Quite a lot of people grow carrots between broad beans because they are tall – the carrot fly only goes 18 inches above the soil. (Chris Luck)

Deep, light loam is the perfect soil for carrots, and think of growing them in a raised bed.

Thinning carrots is time-consuming, but needs to be done regularly, ideally to 50 to 75 mm (2 to 3 in) apart. However, just touching the leaves sends out the strong aroma that attracts carrot fly, so immediately after thinning consider covering the crop with fleece or with the latest fine meshes, sold as 'Enviromesh'. And thin them on a dull day or, if you can, in the evening, as this will minimize the smell. An alternative is to sow the seed in a block and surround it with a barrier of clear polythene about 60 cm (2 ft) high.

I have carrots in a raised bed about a foot all the way round. I found some tubular legs from an old coffee table and draped fleece over. I haven't had any trouble with carrot fly at all. (Maureen Nightingale)

Very early sowings need to be protected with fleece, cloches or their polythene equivalent and kept well watered. Depending on the space you have available, make small sowings of different varieties through the season, right up to August for the latest types.

Without regular water and feeding, carrots may also show signs of splitting, which spoils their looks but not their flavour.

Here are some other good carrot choices.

'Amsterdam Forcing 3'   Long, finger-shaped roots; one of the earliest types for forcing under cloches or polythene

'Chantenay Red Cored 2'	Early maturing, stump-rooted; good on poorer soils
'Nandor'	Crops June to October; stump-rooted
'Parmex'	Round-rooted; good for shallow soils
'Bangor'	Smooth-skinned cylindrical roots; matures in mid season
'Eskimo'	Crops from November to January; tolerant of frost and some carrot fly resistance
'Purple Haze F1'	Vigorous purple roots

Celeriac

Its beautifully mild flavour makes celeriac a wonderful winter vegetable, but it will do well only on the best of soils and must have plenty of moisture so is not ideal for an allotment if you are unable to water very regularly. It also needs a long, unchecked growing season. 'Monarch' and 'Prinz' are varieties widely available.

To get a good crop, start early in the year, sowing the tiny seeds indoors or in a heated greenhouse in late February or early March – they need a temperature of about 10–13ºC (50–55ºF). Because they do not like bare-rooted transplanting, they are best sown in deep modules and thinned to one per cell. Once these have three or four good-sized leaves – this will take up to five weeks – put them outside to harden off before you plant them out.

Celeriac will not thrive if its growth is severely checked, so you need to be sure that the soil is well composted and as water retentive as possible and free from perennial weeds. Use a dibber or trowel to make a hole for each plant and water into the hole before putting in each celeriac, placing them about 23 cm (9 in) apart in each direction (they grow well in a block rather than a row). Make sure that the roots are completely buried and the leaves just resting at soil surface level.

Keep them well watered and as plants develop – from about August onwards – the outer leaves tend to fall flat. Tear these off (you can use them for flavouring, they are good for a soup) to let the sun get to the roots. (Mike Cosgrove)

From then on it is a matter of food, which should be supplied at two- to three-week intervals, water and weeding. A covering of fine mesh or fleece in the early growing stages will help keep carrot fly at bay, and give plants a boost of warmth. Because celeriac is not frost hardy you need to protect roots if you plan to leave them in the ground all winter. A layer of straw offers good protection, though it can also be a haven for slugs and snails.

Parsnips

Parsnips are easy to grow on the allotment as long as you can get the seeds to germinate well and avoid canker, the main disease of this crop. Though they take up a considerable amount of room they will last all winter except through the most severe frosts.

Soil for parsnips should be mildly alkaline (add lime if necessary to correct the pH). Always use fresh seed. Parsnip seed doesn't keep well year to year. Despite what it says on the packet, planting seed in February can be an easy route to failure. Rather, wait until the soil is warm and reasonably dry. Parsnips are slow to germinate and may rot in the soil if conditions are unfavourable. Even later planted seeds will soon catch up. Every parsnip grower has their own experiences:

> *I sowed my parsnips three times and I have about two plants. I think the slugs got them as soon as they showed their little noses. (John Makin)*

> *I don't know why they haven't come up; I think it's just the shape of the soil. You've got to get a fine tilth – they only need to be just half an inch down – not too deep. (Mike Wiffen)*

> *None one year, another year lush foliage and tiny forked roots – I don't know the reason. (Jeanne Mousley).*

Sow seeds where the crop will mature – parsnips don't react well to being transplanted. To avoid canker – a fungal disease that turns roots reddish brown or black, and makes the flesh soggy and unpleasant – choose a resistant variety such as the good old-fashioned 'Tender and True' or the shorter-rooted 'Avonresister'. 'Gladiator' is a reliable F1 hybrid but will give you many fewer seeds for your money.

Allotment gardeners have come up with many ways of getting parsnips to germinate:

Parsnips are quirky. I mix the seeds with wallpaper paste, put it in a plastic bag, cut the corner off and sow it as if you were icing a cake. It contains a fungicide and also gives a consistent temperature and protects the seed. (David Downton)

Or try this:

First put some wet kitchen roll in a container, distribute the seeds evenly over the paper, fit a lid and keep at about 68ºF. Check often, as you want to go to the next stage when the seeds have just germinated and before the roots are too long. Wash the seeds off the paper into a sieve then mix some water-retaining granules with some water and gently add the seed to the gel, which should be thick enough to hold them without sinking. Put the mixture in a plastic bag and squeeze the mixture along a drill. Cover them with soil and keep them well watered. (Tim Callard)

Sow seeds thinly in a groove about 12 mm (½ in) deep, and thin regularly to about 20 cm (8 in) apart. Allow about 30 cm (1 ft) between rows. If carrot fly is a problem on your plot, be prepared for parsnips to be attacked. A covering of fleece or fine mesh may be needed.

With soil rich in organic matter parsnips will only need watering in the very hottest and driest weather. Parsnips can be kept in the ground all winter, and their flavour is said to improve with frost. If it's very icy, cover the tops with fleece or, unless it is likely to be blown away, a thick layer of straw.

Turnips and kohl rabi
TURNIPS

Turnips are not to everyone's taste, but are easy to grow and most palatable, both cooked and raw, when young and tender. Turnips are available in many quick-maturing varieties, and in different colours. Popular choices include the white 'Snowball', crimson and white 'Atlantic' and the yellow 'Golden Ball'. Some varieties, such as 'Aramis', a white root tinted with pale pink, will also stand well without getting too large.

To have a supply of young turnips through the summer it pays to sow seeds little and often every month, beginning in spring. Very early sowings of turnips can be made under polythene or cloches in February, but wait until March to make your first main sowing. Set them about 12 mm (½ in) deep, allowing around 30 cm (1 ft) between rows. Thin them as they mature and (if you like their rather strong taste) use the tops of the thinnings as 'spring greens'. They should eventually be spaced to about 15 cm (6 in) apart.

Turnips seeds, like parsnips, are sensitive to cold.

We tried some turnips – a complete disaster. It was a lot to do with a freezing cold, very dry spell, followed by torrential rain and a dry summer. (Ken Daniels)

They will also need watering well to prevent the tops bolting and the roots becoming tough and woody. If watered sporadically the roots may split. Because they are brassicas, turnips are susceptible to club root. Liming the soil can help this if it is a problem on your plot, and you can also look for seed bred for club root resistance.

Quick-maturing turnips have also been bred to use as a leafy vegetable.

KOHL RABI

Kohl rabi have a mild taste that is a cross between cabbage and turnip and can be eaten raw. They are quick to mature and even easier than turnips. They grow above the soil surface and do not mind being transplanted. Sow seed in small amounts in succession from March to July and you will have them right through until the autumn frosts. Best harvested when small, they come in purple and pale green varieties (some suppliers sell packets of mixed seed) but all have white flesh. Irregular watering will make them split; they are best used small.

We discovered kohl rabi in the eighties, long before they became trendy, and grew them in our Chiswick plot without any problems. But they definitely need to be eaten young. (Ruth)

Swedes

Swedes are vegetables for a large allotment, being greedy of space and inexpensive to buy. They are also said to thrive on neglect:

They say you have to treat them rough – they do better in a field where they're ignored. I hoed them every day and they are quite small – I think I've been giving them too much respect. (Robin Barrett)

Sow seeds in 12-mm (½-in) drills in May, once the weather warms, to give them a good start and to help avoid disease. Select varieties advertised as resistant to club root and mildew such as 'Marian' and 'Ruby'. Thin them as they mature to 23 to 30 cm (9 to 12 in) apart.

Potatoes

Just for their fabulous flavour it's worth making the space for a row of new potatoes. (Ruth)

Potatoes, like runner beans, are signature allotment crops and will live up to their reputation of helping to clear weeds. However, they do take up a lot of space. You also need to have somewhere to store your crop during the winter.

Potatoes come in three main sorts – early, second early and main crop – broadly categorized according to the time they mature. They also vary in the waxiness or flouriness of their flesh and in their colour and shape, as well as in their resistance to attack by scab and other diseases and to wireworm infestation (see the chart on p. 138). With judicious choice of varieties you can have home-grown potatoes on your table from early June. If you order seed potatoes by mail from one of the big commercial suppliers it is difficult to get small quantities – the minimum is usually 3 kg (6½ lb) which will fill two 5- to 6-metre (16- to 19-ft) rows. Look out though for 'taster' packs containing 500 g (1 lb) each of three or four different varieties. If you can, it is much better to visit a local nursery or garden shop and to buy the exact number you need. Many such places will even allow you to buy single seed potatoes to experiment with.

Ideally, you need to have your seed potatoes ready to chit or sprout by late January or early February. Put them nose end up in cardboard boxes or slatted wooden trays and leave them in a cool, light, airy but frost-free place for about six weeks until the sprouts are a good 2–2.5 cm (¾ to 1 in). Don't put them in the dark or the shoots will be long, weak and straggly.

Don't forget to label them – or you'll never know what you've planted. We made that mistake, but only once. (Ruth)

Meanwhile, prepare the soil in your plot. If you have dug and manured in the previous autumn, and possibly dug in shredded paper to improve soil texture, then you will only need to fork it over to remove the worst of the weeds. If you have not, then you can dig in manure as soon as the soil is dry and warm enough to be worked or wait to put it in your trenches.

For very early potatoes, put half a dozen under a cloche or a hoop of plastic in about the middle of February and just let them go. It all depends on the soil – if it's warm enough they will be OK. But you need to watch out for frosts and cover them quick once they're up. (Tim Pryce)

To plant out potatoes, start by using a spade or hoe to make drills (shallow trenches) about 10 cm (4 in) deep placed about 45 cm (18 in) apart for earlies and about 60 cm (2 ft) apart for main crop varieties. You can then fill the trenches with compost or shredded paper – anything to improve both food and water retention.

To find out what works best, this year I put my own compost in one row, leaf mould in another, shredded paper in a third and shop bought compost in a fourth. The ones that did best were the ones with leaf mould, which was a surprise. (Maureen Nightingale)

As you put in each chitted potato (sprout end uppermost) rub off all but the two strongest sprouts with your thumb. If the seed potatoes are very large you can also cut them in two at this stage. Use a hoe or rake to cover each completed row, drawing the soil up to make a small ridge. When the first shoots appear, cover them with soil – again using the hoe or rake. This will ensure that they are deep enough in the soil but also protect them from any late frosts.

It is distressing to arrive at the allotment after an early frost to see the tops of potatoes blackened by frost. On the few times that this has happened we have earthed them up a little and, without exception, new growth has quickly followed. (Ruth)

As the season progresses, carry on earthing up until plants are well grown and you have an unbroken line of foliage. Keep an eye open for any potatoes showing above the soil and cover them at once. Light will turn them green and make them inedible. Apart from that there is nothing else you need do except for watering in very dry spells and possibly removing any large weeds that spring up alongside or between your rows. It takes at least 12 weeks for a potato crop to mature.

Wireworms are a common pest of potatoes (see p. 94), but of the diseases that attack potatoes by far the most serious is potato blight. Before the potatoes below ground are mature the leaves, attacked by a fungus, become criss-crossed with fungal threads. These are particularly prominent in wet weather, which encourages fungal growth. In the worst cases, the top growth blackens and dies back prematurely and the potatoes rot below ground. When blight is less severe it is possible to save the crop by digging it up as soon as you can, though it is wise not to bank on the crop keeping well over the winter. On an allotment this is also neighbourly. Once spores start blowing around the plot and getting into the soil they can linger there and affect crops in subsequent years.

When blight struck we took the advice of the plot 'experts' and immediately cut the tops off all our potatoes. We lost a few of the first earlies but all the rest were fine. Others who left it later weren't so lucky. (Ruth)

There are ways of discouraging blight, for instance:

When planting new potatoes put rhubarb leaves in the bottom of the trench – it helps to prevent blight. (Pat Bence)

EXTRA CROPS

What was left of last year's potatoes I put in in June and we had new potatoes in September. And they didn't get the blight. (Doug Chainey)

New potatoes for Christmas and the New Year are also a possibility with the new varieties such as 'Carlingford' and 'Bambino' bred to be planted in July. These late-planting (second-crop) varieties are, in fact, springtime seed potatoes that have been stored at low temperatures. You can plant them straight into the ground without the need for chitting and they will be ready to lift from late October, or as soon as the foliage is fully grown.

Or there may be no need to buy in potatoes specially:

When you dig your new potatoes put some in dry compost in a sealed biscuit tin and bury them. They will come out six months later (for Christmas) in perfect condition; you will even be able to scrape them. (Tim Callard)

One year, we somehow managed to throw a whole lot of substandard potatoes into the compost heap. They sprouted brilliantly and in July we dug out a superb collection of new potatoes. (Ruth)

There are dozens of potato varieties – just experiment to find the ones you like best:

I was told that the best potato is 'Yukon Gold'. I've grown them this year – they have a fantastic flavour. They're a brilliant all-round potato. (David Downton)

SOME OTHER POTATO VARIETIES TO TRY
First earlies
'Rocket'	Earliest of all; soft, waxy white flesh
'Belle de Fontenay'	Pale cream, waxy flesh
'Pentland Javelin'	White, waxy flesh

Second earlies
'Nadine'	High-yielding, good disease resistance; white flesh
'Maris Peer'	Creamy flesh
'Charlotte'	Tender, pale yellow flesh; good salad potato

Main crop
'Pentland Javelin'	White flesh; good all-purpose variety

'King Edward'   Old classic; cream flesh; good all rounder
'Desirée'   Red-skinned; pale yellow flesh
'Cara'   White with pink eyes, white flesh; ideal for baking
'Valor'   White-skinned; keeps well
'Pink Fir Apple'   Knobbly, pink skin; waxy, creamy flesh

Sweet potatoes

A warming climate, and the increasing availability of ever more exotic vegetables, has made sweet potatoes a perfectly feasible crop. Unlike ordinary potatoes they are not chitted, but raised from sprouted offshoots or 'slips' which you have to buy. They need to be planted in pots of compost to root, then set out as for ordinary potatoes. They will yield about five or six tubers per plant.

You have to start early and shelter them – they don't seem to be troubled by pests. They are super. They are quite expensive but worth it. (Sue Bryant)

You can try cutting up tubers to make your own slips – they need to be forced indoors – but don't bank on this being successful.

Jerusalem artichokes

The tall shoots that grow from knobbly Jerusalem artichokes make a good border along the side of an allotment where they will be reasonably economical on space. Like potatoes, they are planted as tubers, though unlike them they do not need to be chitted. Also, they can be left in the ground all winter and harvested as needed. They definitely have their disadvantages:

They're a bit of a pest. You put in a row and before you know it they're 3 feet wide. And they're such a bother to scrape and prepare. (Robin Barrett).

Artichoke tubers need planting about 10 cm (4 in) deep and 30 cm (12 in) apart and the soil raked up to form a ridge. As the tops emerge and start to grow, they can be earthed up some more. Ideally, the shoots, which can reach 2 m (6 ft 3 in) in height, may need to be tied up to stop them being blown over by the wind or rocking, both of which will bring the tubers up to the surface. Metal wire strung between sturdy canes is a good method.

Jerusalem artichokes are not to everyone's liking. While delicate in taste, they can cause severe flatulence and are fiddly to prepare. To cut down on work, select a large smooth-skinned variety such as 'Fuseau'. Whatever sort you choose, begin digging them in autumn, after you have cut the stems back to about 30 cm (1 ft).

At Highgate we inherited a clump of artichokes which, despite our best efforts at digging them out came up reliably year after year. The crop was not large – enough for three or four batches of soup – but were all we wanted or needed. (Ruth)

THE ONION FAMILY

All members of the onion family share a need for plenty of food (they are 'greedy feeders') and susceptibility to the same diseases. They are most satisfying to grow; properly ripened, dried and stored, onion, shallot and garlic crops will keep you going well into the spring.

Onions and their relations are all susceptible to white rot, a fungus that invades and rots the bulbs and is particularly prevalent in cold, damp weather. You may be able to take steps to avoid it:

Pour semi-skimmed milk along your drills. This promotes a flush of beneficial fungus at onion root level that fends off the white rot causing fungus. (Tim Callard)

What's important if you have this problem is to burn any affected material (or dispose of it safely) and, if possible, avoid growing any members of the onion family in that soil for several years. Be careful, too, not to spread the fungus on your hands.

It is a horrible and disappointing sight to dig up a crop and find it mushy with the fungus. (Ruth)

Another cause of problems is infestation by the maggots of the onion fly. If you're well prepared and/or notice the problem in time you may be able to save the crop by dusting with derris or pyrethrum or using an insecticide. The best deterrent is to cover your crop with fleece or very fine netting, as you would to keep off carrot fly.

> Up to last year we've never had onion fly – they have a maggot in them. You need to spray them early on. (Doug Chainey)

Onions and shallots

Although they can be grown from seed, onions are really easy to raise from mini heat-treated bulbs or 'sets'. They need well-cultivated, loose soil, not too recently manured, and a sunny spot. If you have the space you may want to grow red and white varieties, such as 'Red Baron' and 'White Prince', as well as the regular sorts like 'Autumn Gold', 'Sturon' and 'Stuttgart Giant'. For size, and for showing, choose 'Showmaster'.

As long as it is not too cold or wet, onion sets can go into the ground in March. Put them into holes made with a dibber or narrow trowel, set so that the point is just below the soil surface to help prevent birds pulling them up. They need to be about 15 cm (6 in) apart. If they push up as they begin to grow (the developing roots can sometimes make them do this) just push them gently back in. Discard any that are soft or show signs of mould.

> Just an inch and a half between sets can make all the difference. If they're too close red onions just shoot off whereas white varieties don't seem to. (Simon Hewitt)

Through the growing season keep the onions weeded and watered when necessary, and well fed, either with liquid feed or an occasional top dressing. You can buy a specially formulated onion fertilizer for the purpose.

> We are now lucky to be able to buy loose sets from local suppliers, so we can start with as many as we need. The sets we bought in packs of 100 by mail order were always successful, though we usually ended up with more than we needed. At the

end of the row we put some in close together and harvested them early as 'mega' spring onions. (Ruth)

For a very early crop you can grow winter onions, planting them in October. Look for varieties such as 'Radar' (white) and 'Electric' (red).

I've taken to growing winter onions. They're no trouble but they don't keep. (Sue Bryant)

Alternatively, onions – including so-called pickling or silverskin onions – can be grown from seed planted in pots or pans of seed compost. Sow overwintering varieties in August or indoors, or germinate seed in a warm greenhouse in early January or direct into the allotment in March. The advantage of these is that they are more resistant to bolting.

SPRING ONIONS

I sow the seed quite thickly and pull the thinnings as I need them. They are a great stand-by. (Ruth)

It's good to have a supply of spring onions all year. For early pickings, sow seed in September – plants are hardy enough to survive most winter weather. You can then put more seed under a cloche in February, and make another sowing in May or June. As well as the regular white types, such as the ever popular 'Guardsman' and 'White Lisbon' you can also get seeds of pretty red varieties like 'Furio'.

SHALLOTS

Prized by cooks for their mild flavour, and also for pickling, shallots are grown in a similar way to onion sets, but can be put in during February. They need to be planted less deeply – leave the tip of the bulb protruding. By July the original single bulb will have multiplied and the tops withered. They can then be lifted out.

When we had more room we grew shallots and stored them in the shed. They have a lovely flavour. (Ruth)

WELSH ONIONS

Also called everlasting onions, these are usually started from young plants planted 23 cm (9 in) apart, in March and April, which grow into clumps that look like bunches of spring onions. They can also be grown from seed. As long as the whole clump isn't gathered, the few remaining onions will continue to produce more stems.

Garlic

'Plant on the shortest day and harvest on the longest' is the old adage for growing garlic, although experience says that late October or early November are much better months for planting as this gives the plants longer to get going before the coldest weather sets in.

Prepare your ground then divide up the garlic heads into individual cloves. Place the cloves where you want them – about 23 cm (9 in) apart in all directions in rows or blocks – then use a sharp-pointed trowel to make individual holes into which each can be popped. Make the holes just deep enough that the tip of the clove is still projecting above the ground. Three fat heads will give you about 20 cloves.

In spring, when the plants are growing well, garlic will appreciate a top dressing of compost or concentrated manure. At this point you also need to begin to weed regularly, and water in very dry spells.

We usually buy our garlic from a specialist supplier or nursery, but in years when we've left it very late we've grown garlic almost as good from heads we have bought in the supermarket. In the end it seems that the way you cultivate it is what's most important. (Ruth)

As well as 'ordinary' garlic you can also grow 'Elephant' garlic which is not a true garlic but produces huge cloves and a mild flavour.

Leeks

Leeks get better with the cold. (Doug Chainey)

Hardy and versatile, leeks are a justifiable allotment favourite and economical on space. Of the established varieties, try 'Musselburgh' for short, thick stems or 'Lyon Prizetaker' for long, white ones. Also reliable, though more expensive, are the F1s such as 'Carlton' and 'Oarsman' bred to reduce the slight swelling or 'bulbing' that can occur at the stem bases.

Leek seeds can be begun in a seedbed at your plot or at home in containers in February or March. Sow them as thinly as you can, but if they look overcrowded as they germinate thin them or pot them on to give you a good selection of healthy seedlings 15–20 cm (6–8 in) tall. These can then be put into their permanent bed, which needs to have been well manured the previous year.

The traditional way to plant leeks is to make holes about 15 cm (6 in) deep with a dibber, trim the top off each plant then put one plant in each hole, fill the hole with water and leave them.

If you find you need to transplant them when they're smaller, leeks will actually grow very well planted in deep holes with a trowel or dibber in the normal way. (Ruth)

Leeks are by reputation 'greedy feeders' and will need plenty of food during their growing season as well as water in dry spells. A midsummer top dressing of concentrated manure is a good idea, as is earthing them up a little with the hoe as you weed to give you as much blanched stem as possible.

As well as the usual onion family problems, leeks are prone to rust. If mild, you can just remove affected leaves as you harvest, but badly affected plants may have to be ditched. Don't put these on the compost heap – burn them or deposit them somewhere safe.

VEGETABLE FRUITS

From outsize marrows to superb-tasting tomatoes, vegetable fruits are the pride of the allotment, while courgettes are notorious for their fecundity. Most of these vegetables originate in warm, wet climates and need treatment to match, as well as food to nurture them. It pays to prepare the ground thoroughly, adding loads of organic matter, well before you begin to sow the seeds. The most tender of vegetable fruits, such as peppers and aubergines, will do well outdoors only in the height of a hot summer. Otherwise they need the protection of a greenhouse, cloches or a cold frame and, of course, protection from slugs and snails.

Courgettes and marrows

Just keep watering marrows. They like manure. When we put them where we had our manure heap they did really well. (Angela Downs)

For courgettes you have the choice of the regular 'Zucchini' or 'Green Bush', or the pale green Lebanese 'Clarita'. 'Gold Rush' and 'Orelia' have bright yellow fruit which though they look pretty don't have quite the flavour of the green sorts. 'Eight Ball' are round. Marrows are the quintessential allotment vegetables, but not as popular nowadays as courgettes. They come in two types, the bush varieties such as 'Long Green Bush 4' and the early 'Tiger Cross' and the trailing 'Table Dainty' and 'Long Green Trailing'.

You can sow seeds straight into the ground in mid May, but a more reliable method is to raise these vegetables indoors in the warmth, beginning in late April. You can do this in pots or, even better, cells. Experience shows that germination is best if seeds are planted horizontally. This seems to encourage roots, then shoots, to emerge more easily.

When planting out, allow plenty of space between plants – 1 m (3 ft) at least – and consider using matting collars or a bark mulch (added after rain) to help water retention if you are liable to be unable to water your crop frequently. Trailing marrows will need another 1.2 m (4 ft) of space to expand in.

In fear of failure we always manage to plant out an extra courgette plant (or two) with the good intention of pulling up the spare if all the plants flourish. Somehow this very rarely happens, leaving us with extra courgettes even over and above the usual surpluses. (Ruth)

As the season progresses you may find that the leaves become mildewed, but this does not seem to affect the crop.

Our courgettes were like Triffids last year. This year they were straggly then, after a few days of sun, they were completely transformed. You can't give them away around here. (Ken Daniels)

The most serious problem that can affect courgettes is cucumber mosaic virus, which mottles and stunts leaves and fruits, though most varieties are now bred with good viral resistance.

Marrows need less attention, but if you plan to enter 'heaviest marrow' in your local show, nip off smaller fruits to concentrate the plants' energies into one or two super specimens.

We experimented one year with the spaghetti marrow. Although it grew wonderfully we absolutely hated the texture of the inner 'strings' when they were cooked. (Ruth)

Squashes and pumpkins

I try to grow one plant of three or four different varieties so I don't get a glut. (Vicky Scott)

As well as being great fun to grow, squashes and pumpkins have the great advantage that if sound they will keep indoors in a cool place all winter. They are basically grown in the same way as marrows and courgettes and, like them, need to be set at least 1 m (3 ft) apart. If you are growing just one or two plants you can even put them direct into a pile of compost. They will love the food, moisture and warmth that this provides.

I've planted squashes and courgettes on a ridge of topsoil topped with grass cuttings, which gives food as well as warmth. They are wonderful. (Maureen Nightingale)

Another alternative, for smaller fruited sorts, is to grow them up a trellis strung between poles, as for runner beans (see p. 109).

To get good fruiting, it helps to nip out the tips of the shoots once they are about 45 cm (18 in) long, so stimulating the growth of laterals. If fruit do not seem to be forming well, you may need to assist pollination by transferring pollen from male to female flowers with a paintbrush. The female flowers are the ones with slightly swollen bases.

When successful, squashes and pumpkins can achieve giant proportions and quantities, and huge vigour:

We had Mandan squashes like rugby footballs or even bigger. And we got 27 butternut squashes from one plant – even the smallest was 4 or 5 inches long. (Ken Daniels)

They [pumpkins] are about 20 feet from where the root is. They just go where they want. You think you have a good one fertilized and then one appears somewhere else. (Robin Barrett)

To stop developing fruit being damaged by pests, or just rotting on the ground, it helps to support them on pieces of stone or even small shelves made by putting pieces of wood on top of upturned flowerpots. Stripping away a few of the leaves around each fruit will allow in more sunlight for ripening.

As well as the huge pumpkins, such as the aptly named 'Hundredweight' and 'Big Max', you can get smaller fruited ones like 'Becky' or miniatures such as 'Jack Be Little'. For squashes there is a choice of dozens of shapes and colours, including butternuts, acorns, patty pans and custards as well as the more unusual onion squash and the pimply 'Hubbard'.

Tomatoes

When they fruit successfully allotment tomatoes have unique taste, so it is always worth planting a few and keeping your fingers crossed. (Ruth)

Allotment tomatoes can be hit and miss, depending on the weather and the threat of blight. They can also suffer if you aren't able to get to the plot to water and feed them regularly. If you are growing from seed, start outdoor tomato varieties indoors on a windowsill or in the warmth of a heated greenhouse at a temperature of around 18–21°C (65–75°F) any time from mid February to mid April. (If you miss out you can always buy ready-grown plants.) Sow seeds in good compost and cover them to just 6 mm (¼ inch), then keep them warm and moist, though be careful not to overwater them as they are prone to damping off. Move them around as need be to stop them growing lopsidedly towards the light.

Once the seedlings are large enough to handle, transplant them into individual 75 mm (3 in) pots and harden them off. It is best not to put them into the allotment until plants are good and strong, with five leaves, or when you can see the first signs of flower buds forming. Wait, of course, until there is no risk of frost.

> *When I put them in I scoop up the soil around them with both hands, then make a depression all around, so the water runs out not down. And a little blood and bonemeal. (Mike Wiffen)*

While it is perfectly fine to plant tomatoes direct into well-composted allotment soil, ideally in a sunny, sheltered spot, you can help to ward off diseases by putting them into deep 19 cm (7½ in) pots, sterilized before filling, and either placed on a path or paved area or sunk into the ground. (If this is your choice, you may want to grow one of the varieties bred specifically for containers, see below.) Even this is not always successful, however.

> *I've got a lot of problems with my tomatoes – blossom end rot. The calcium is leeching out because they're in pots. It's infrequent watering that does it. (Reg Simmons)*

Or you can put several plants in one large urn-type container, or use growing bags.

> *Cut a growbag in half and stand it on end for tomatoes. It holds water very well. (Tim Pryce)*

To give them a good start you may want to cover tomato plants with individual bell-shaped cloches or an equivalent you've rigged up with pieces of plastic.

Tomatoes need plenty of water and food, especially potash. Without regular watering, fruit are liable to split. They will also suffer from blossom end rot, which creates nasty brown or black patches on the base of the fruit. To help water retention it is useful to surround the base of each plant with a good mulch; if you are growing them in pots or bags, mix in some 'swell gel' granules to assist with this – or you can use it direct in the soil.

When I planted my tomatoes, I dug a hole and in the bottom of each put a tablespoon of 'swell gel'. Now [at the end of the season] they have only been watered three times and I've had no splitting or blossom end rot. (Maureen Nightingale)

Once fruit start to form tomatoes need feeding every 10 to 14 days. You can use one of the specially formulated tomato fertilizers (dilute and apply as per instructions) or make your own from comfrey or nettles cut and soaked for a week or two in water. The foul-smelling solution then needs to be diluted about 1 part to 10 with water.

I brew comfrey up for a week then take the rotting leaves off and put them on the compost before I use it. (Maureen Nightingale)

As they grow, tomatoes will need tying to 1.5 m (5 ft) cane supports. Use soft string, not wire, or you will damage the tender stems. On a windy allotment two canes, set opposite each other, are helpful for added support. The other care that tomato plants need depends on the type you are growing. While 'regular' (technically cordon) sorts need their side shoots removing regularly, to leave four to six trusses, with the top shoot taken out to 'stop' the plant once these have formed, bush types do not need this treatment.

Because allotment sites are so open, allowing fungal spores to fly readily around in the air, allotment tomatoes seem to be particularly prone to blight, especially in wet summers that encourage fungal growth.

Tomato blight struck quickly, and even spraying with Bordeaux mixture didn't save them. Fast forward 12 months, to a warmer, drier summer. Keeping a watchful eye open, and taking off any blackened leaves, we had a reasonable crop. (Ruth)

It may be possible to avoid the worst of the blight by being at the ready:

We have had some blight and when I see a leaf with a mark on it I take it off and burn it. (Maureen Nightingale)

And blight goes on and on ...

We've had it here for seven years. It's always when they're green and just ready to ripen. (Reg, Highgate)

The bonus of outdoor tomatoes is that they are much less likely than greenhouse-grown ones to be infested with whitefly. They can also be attacked by viruses, which turn the leaves of tomato plants yellow and mottled and, if extreme, make plants wilted, stunted and unfruitful. Apart from choosing virus-resistant varieties, and maximizing plant care, there is little that can be done about such attacks.

These tomato varieties are some good choices for allotment cultivation.

'Ailsa Craig'	Old-fashioned heavy cropper
'Money Maker'	Reliable, popular; medium-sized fruits
'Marmande'	Mediterranean, large 'beefsteak'-style fruit
'Sweet Million'	Bush type; many small, sweet fruits
'Sungold'	Small, cherry-type orange fruit
'Tornado'	Early type, bred for English summer conditions
'Tumbler'	Bush type, bred for container growing
'Mirabelle'	Bright yellow cherry tomatoes; bush type
'Tropical Ruby'	Baby 'plum' tomatoes; can be grown as bush or cordon type

Cucumbers and gherkins

Although they can be quite tricky to get started and established, just three or four healthy plants will give you enough cucumbers to feed a family from July right through until September.

Three good varieties for an allotment are 'Marketmore', 'Burpless Tasty Green' and 'Long Green Ridge'. Or try the unusual yellow (and lemon-shaped) 'Crystal Lemon' or 'Sunsweet'. All cucumber seed needs starting off in pots or cells, either in the warmth indoors in late April – or outdoors in a sunny spot in mid May. Because seedlings are very prone to damping off it is vital not to overwater. If disease does strike, then start again in different pots and try more warmth and less water.

We've learnt from experience that cucumber plants can keel over in a matter of hours. Even when put out into the allotment under fleece there are nearly always some casualties. (Ruth)

You need to be sure that you are past the period of frost risk before planting out cucumbers. They will enjoy their own 'heap':

I use spent mushroom compost. I put half of that and half of soil to grow cucumbers. I've had a cucumber in every leaf axil. As you take them off another one comes. I'll just put in one plant next year. (Reg Simmons)

Some gardeners favour planting through a water-retentive membrane, though this has the disadvantage of getting very hot in high summer. Whatever method you favour, plants need to be about 60 cm (2 ft) apart.

Once plants start to take off strongly, consider supporting them in some way to save space and to help keep fruit off the ground. Strong wires strung between stakes work well, as does a wicker wigwam. Or you can improvise.

We had great success with an old metal frame that had once been part of a mini greenhouse. The cucumbers spread themselves all over it and it gave them plenty of sun. (Ruth)

Cucumbers will appreciate the shade cast, say, by a runner bean crop during some part of the day. A general feed will be fine, but cucumbers will relish the high nitrogen supplied by regular sprinklings of bone meal. Rather than letting plants get over large and straggly, you can pinch out the growing tips once you have a good quantity of flowers.

To keep cucumber plants growing into the space I want, rather than straggling over everything around, I 'funnel' them between two 15 cm (6 in) pieces of stick placed on either side of the stems. (Ruth)

If you like pickles, gherkins are well worth a try. They can be grown exactly like cucumbers.

Peppers and chillies

Although the fruits of outdoor allotment peppers (capsicums) and chillies may not be as big as those of greenhouse-grown specimens they will be packed with flavour. Hot summers are best for them.

Good allotment choices for peppers from seed are varieties like 'Unicorn' and 'Jumbo' which turn from green to red when ripe, or you can choose 'Carnival Mixture' which will give you a range of colours including orange and deep purple. For chillies, anything called 'Jalapeno' will be relatively mild. Hottest are the small, intensely flavoured types such as 'Hot Mexican' and 'Ring of Fire' and scotch bonnet chillies such as 'Big Sun'.

Start peppers and chillies off in the warmth – they need temperatures of 18–21ºC (65–70ºF). They will do well in cells or small pots, and will need potting on at least once before they are big enough – and the weather warm enough – for them to be put outdoors in the hottest, sunniest place you have available. To stop plants getting straggly, nip out the tops once they are about 30 cm (12 in) high. They will appreciate feeding with a tomato fertilizer. In a cold, wet summer they may be susceptible to rotting stems or may just not make flowers early enough in the season to give you any fruit.

Until they had flowers on them, we kept the chilli plants we'd been given under cloches, making sure they had plenty of water. Once uncovered they quickly began making fruit. (Ruth)

Aubergines

I've got some in the greenhouse – they were advertised as 'gigantic'. They are not that big yet. (Sue Bryant)

With an allotment greenhouse aubergines, with their lovely glossy purple fruits, are well worth trying, and they may even do well under cloches or in a cold frame if you are prepared to experiment and the weather is kind. 'Black Beauty' and 'Moneymaker' are two reliable varieties or you could try one of the unusual white varieties such as 'Mohican'.

Start aubergines off in February or March at a temperature of at least 21°C (70°F). Plants need to be at a minimum of 16°C (61°F) as the plants mature. Use 75 mm (3 in) pots and put two or three seeds in each pot; you can then remove the two weakest ones. When you pot them on, make sure you plant them deeply, with the first leaf at soil level. You can then either leave them in these 18 cm (7 in) pots or transfer them to allotment soil about 45 cm (18 in) apart or similarly spaced in a growing bag.

When plants are about 23 cm (9 in) high, pinch out the growing tips to encourage bushy growth. Once a fruit has formed on a branch, pinch off the tip of that branch, leaving three leaves beyond it, to prevent the plant putting maximum energy into fruit formation. On an allotment you will do best if you restrict each plant to about four fruits, which may mean pinching out side shoots too.

Otherwise, you need to keep plants well watered and, ideally, in conditions that will encourage the humidity they prefer, which will also help to deter red spider mites, the only serious aubergine attacker. A weekly feed with a tomato feed is also necessary.

My aubergines are not doing too well. We have been away and they are lacking rain. (Andrew Malleson)

Sweetcorn

Sweetcorn will do well in an allotment provided it has plenty of sun, water and a regular supply of food throughout its growing season. You also need to remember to set out seeds and plants in a block, not a row, to allow the pollen from the male flowers at the top of the plant the best chance of fertilizing the female tassels below. You can choose 'standard' varieties such as 'Sundance', but the latest varieties are marketed under names such as 'Supersweet' and 'Tender Sweet' and include 'Early Extra Sweet' and 'Swift'.

The seeds of sweetcorn need plenty of warmth to germinate but once up will speed away. You can wait until mid May before you sow seeds direct into the plot or, if you wish, begin them in April indoors. If you do this, enclose each pot in a polythene bag and put it in the airing cupboard until the seeds germinate, then uncover them and transfer them to a sunny windowsill.

We've had mixed success with sweetcorn but because it needs watering when small and my attention is unpredictable it can be a problem. My wife started seedlings off in our garden shed and couldn't understand why there was so much damage – it was a hedgehog who in other respects was very welcome. I found it had climbed into a box. (Edward Probert)

Final spacing needs to be about 30 cm (1 ft) between plants. To concentrate growth into the cobs, nip off any side shoots that appear. The cobs are ready to harvest when the tassels have turned brown and are usually disease free.

Squirrels love sweetcorn as we discovered to our cost. Though not caught in the act it was not hard to imagine them stripping our lovely cobs bare with their sharp teeth. After that we made a netting cage around the crop. (Ruth)

You can also buy seeds such as 'Minipop', bred to give the best baby corn, ideal for Chinese dishes. These are grown in the same way but harvested just when the female tassels begin to show and before they are pollinated.

Globe artichokes

We had an artichoke 'hedge' at the end of the allotment for a while, but it was huge. In the end we decided that raspberries were a better use of the space. (Ruth)

Globe artichokes are an oddity because their edible parts are in fact the 'chokes' or hearts that form the flower bases, and the swollen bases of the leafy bracts around them. These big plants with their grey-green leaves work well as attractive plot dividers. 'Green Globe' is the most popular and widely grown variety, but 'Violetto di Choggia' with purple heads is even better looking.

You can buy globe artichokes ready grown, but if you prefer to start from seeds these are best begun indoors, above 10°C (50°F) then potted on and planted out in well-manured soil in spring, leaving at least 1 m (3 ft) between each. They need plenty of water and a generous spring mulch of compost, though will not usually make globes – unopened flowers – until their second year (and any flowers that form in the first year are best removed to strengthen growth). To maximize the number of heads, cut off small ones as they form and cook and eat them whole, to leave four to six flowers on each head.

I've been successful with globe artichokes. I have to drag my husband down to pick the small ones I can't reach so that we get some big ones. (Vicky Scott)

Because they only live five or six years, replace the weakest plants each year. Slice off side shoots (suckers) with roots attached from strong plants in April or May and put them direct into their permanent positions. The remainder of the plant can be discarded.

CHAPTER 4

SALAD LEAVES, HERBS AND FLOWERS

For taste, colour and interest – and lots of quick, easy growing – salads, herbs and flowers will brighten up the allotment, the kitchen and the home. Choose those you like to eat and experiment with herbs of different flavours to mix and match with your favourite foods. As well as being decorative, some allotment flowers are also edible and many make good companion plants for vegetables, helping flower fertilization and pest control.

SALAD LEAVES

With good planning it is possible to have salad leaves of some kind from the allotment in almost every week of the year, especially in mild winters, though it pays to protect winter salads such as radicchio with fleece. For most salad vegetables, 'little and often' is the watchword for sowing, since most mature quickly and it is easy to get overrun with excesses. All need well-manured soil that retains water well. Equally, all are prone to attack by slugs and snails, rabbits and any other animals partial to tasty leaves.

Lettuce

How can it be possible to have a glut of lettuces every year! There are so many different sorts, and the seeds germinate so readily, that by July there is more lettuce than we can possibly eat or even give away. (Ruth)

So much for the theory – and discipline – of sowing lettuce little and often. Indoors, you can start lettuce seeds off in pots as early as February; they will need the protection of a cold frame, cloche or fleece when you plant them while there is still a risk of frost. By mid March or early April they will germinate readily without additional heat. Because they transplant well, you don't need to sow seed *in situ*; work around whatever is convenient, depending on the space available.

> *Before thinning or transplanting I've found it pays to soak the ground with water beforehand and afterwards – a technique called puddling we've nicknamed 'the paddy field approach'. (Ruth)*

Above all, lettuce needs plenty of water. Setting plants quite close together also helps water retention, as does keeping them covered with fleece while they establish themselves. Allowed to dry out, lettuces will quickly bolt, though keeping them thoroughly and constantly damp is an added attraction to slugs and snails.

For flavour, there are few lettuces to beat the butterhead 'Tom Thumb', the cos-style 'Little Gem' and the crisp 'Webb's Wonderful', but there are lots of others to choose from, including the 'All the Year Round' (a butterhead that can also be planted in September and overwintered), Romaines such as 'Claremont' and various icebergs. Red varieties include the cos-type 'Pandero'. Or try buying a packet of mixed seeds and see what you get.

If space is at a premium, and you can't be on hand to water as frequently, good choices are the 'cut and come again' types, like 'Salad Bowl' and the colourful 'Red Salad Bowl' from which you harvest the lower leaves. 'Lolla Rossa', with deep maroon leaves, is another good picking lettuce. 'Cardinale' will also make small hearts.

For the earliest of all lettuce, sow seeds of winter hardy varieties like 'Valdor' and 'Winter Density' *in situ* in August or September and thin out rather than transplanting. Even with some protection you are unlikely to get 100% survival, but it is worth the effort to have home-grown salad the following spring.

Rocket

Wild rocket germinates and grows much more slowly than the annual type, so don't give up on it. Once established it will self-seed. With some persistence I now have a whole collection of productive plants. (Ruth)

Rocket is expensive to buy and quick to grow. Easiest to cultivate is annual rocket, which will even overwinter if sown in autumn. In late summer, it will mature in a month, though in mid season will quickly run to seed. Ideally, sow seeds little and often. The seeds are tiny and hard to sow thinly so you need to pull and eat the thinnings.

Wild rocket, which has a stronger flavour, is a short-lived perennial with smaller, darker leaves, which can be picked as you need them.

Both types of rocket need plenty of water. If you want perfect leaves you will need to protect them from flea beetle (see p. 95), though so-called Turkish rocket is advertised as having some beetle resistance.

Chinese cabbage

Big, hearty, tight-packed white heads make Chinese cabbage an excellent autumn salad – sow seeds direct into the ground in May and June and thin plants out to about 15 cm (6 in) apart. It stands well, and is slow to bolt even in dry spells. Its biggest problem is that it is extremely prone to attacks by both whitefly and slugs.

Lovely leaves, horrible slugs. (Ruth)

Salad mixes and oriental greens

One of the best autumn crops. I always grow these. (Ruth)

These are grown in the same way as either spinach or mizuna (see p. 121). To be eaten raw as salad they need to be picked when very young – or use the thinnings. There is a wide range of mixes available, from baby leaves (rocket, various lettuces and corn salad) to Italian salad blends, which also include basil, red-ribbed dandelion and salad bowl lettuce. Mesclun mixes feature lots of spicy flavoured leaves such as 'Koto' spinach, which can also be grown on its own. Many are 'cut and come again', giving extra value.

Radicchio

Purple radicchio leaves have a slightly bitter taste. Because seeds are best planted in late summer (to prevent bolting), they follow well in the space left once broad beans or mangetout have been harvested. 'Palla Rossa Bella' is a reliably good variety. To help water conservation, and to renew the fertility of the soil, manure the ground well before you sow. In mid season, concentrated manure is handy for this purpose.

You can either sow radicchio seeds where plants will mature and thin them out, or sow them in a seedbed and transplant them. For final positioning allow about 23 cm (9 in) between plants. Do not worry if the crop looks very green to begin with. As the days begin to shorten in autumn they will redden and the plants begin to heart up. Ideally, they need to be protected from frost with fleece or a cloche to prolong the season.

Even when the outer leaves look mushy and horrible in the middle of winter you can find good, edible hearts within. (Ruth)

Chicory

Growing chicory takes almost a whole year of cultivation, but is worth the effort if you love to have fresh, crisp winter salads. For the traditional white heads you also need a warm, dark place to keep it in while the pale heads or chicons are forming.

To grow chicory well – it has long, penetrating roots – you need a rich soil, ideally well manured. Choose seed such as 'Apollo' or 'F1 Witloof Zoom' and sow it thinly, direct into the plot, in late spring, and thin plants to about 23 cm (9 in) apart. By October or November the leaves will have died down and can be cut off within about 5 cm (2 in) of the base. Dig up the roots, remove any side shoots and trim the tapered ends to leave roots about 20 cm (8 in) long. These can now be stored in a frost-free shed until you are ready to use them. Plant up four at a time to a 20-cm (8-in) pot, cover with black polythene and bring them indoors. Left in a dark cupboard at about 14ºC (55ºF) for three or four weeks they will sprout their chicons, which can then be cut off and eaten.

Living in a flat meant it was difficult to find a space for ambitious projects like chicory forcing. In one mild winter we successfully forced some in the allotment shed, keeping the pots surrounded with newspaper to keep them as warm as possible. (Ruth)

Sorrel

The leaves of sorrel look rather like spinach but have a sharper, much more acid taste. Best for eating is the French or buckler-leafed sorrel which, because it is perennial, needs a permanent place in the plot. Ideally, sorrel likes some shade, so can thrive under a tree. You need to prevent it from drying out as this makes the leaves taste very bitter (they also get more bitter as they age).

Sorrel seeds germinate best only above 7ºC (45ºF), so for early pickings they need to be started off indoors in early spring or outdoors once the weather has warmed up. You can begin them in a seedbed and transplant or start them off *in situ*, but you will eventually need to allow about 30 cm (1 ft) between mature plants. You should be able to pick young leaves right through the growing season, until flowering.

Like other herbaceous perennials sorrel is easy to lift and divide in autumn. It will appreciate a good mulch in the spring.

A few sorrel plants along the allotment edge lasted the ten years we had the Highgate plot. The leaves were definitely best when young. (Ruth)

Corn salad

Also known as lamb's lettuce or, from the French, *mâche*, corn salad is a mild, slightly nutty-tasting salad and easy to grow. Like rocket it is expensive to buy. Look for large-leafed varieties and sow seed outside in late summer for autumn and winter salads and in early spring for summer ones. Overwintering plants, though frost hardy, will appreciate the protection of a cloche or fleece, against both the cold and the wet.

Because seeds can be slow to germinate, they will do best if you soak them in water overnight before planting them in shallow drills. Otherwise, apart from the ravages of slugs and snails, they are trouble free – all they need is some thinning and regular watering.

We've tried corn salad but decided that it didn't have much flavour and wasn't worth the space. (Ruth)

Land cress

For a peppery taste, similar to watercress, land cress (also known as American or winter cress) is easy to grow. Seed can be sown in spring for summer leaves or in autumn to use over the winter. For germination, land cress seeds need plenty of water, so soak the ground well before sowing. After germination, thin plants to about 20 cm (8 in) apart.

ALLOTMENT HERBS

I love having herbs at the allotment – there's always something to enjoy and to use for cooking. (Ruth)

You can make a proper herb garden or scatter your herbs in vacant spaces around the plot – or do some of each. The advantage of herbs is that many are attractive to bees and butterflies as well as adding extra flavour to your cooking. Some, like rosemary, bay and mint, will need permanent places – ideally, where they will not impede the growth of other plants. To chime with their origins, most need lots of sun. Soft-leafed sorts, like basil and parsley, need good protection from slugs and snails.

Parsley, though botanically a biennial, will need sowing afresh every year, while basil, coriander and the annual herbs should be sown several times a year to give you a regular supply for the kitchen. As a rule, the leaves of flowering herbs have the most subtle flavour just before the blooms emerge. After flowering they are much more pungent.

Rosemary

A single rosemary bush is all you need on the allotment. Though not fussy about soil, it will appreciate a sheltered spot, as against the sunny side of a shed, where it will flower in spring. It is easiest to start off with a small plant from a nursery and, once established, it will grow quickly. Just give it a good cut-back once a year after it has flowered.

To renew an old rosemary bush, or propagate one, take cuttings of half ripe shoots in summer and keep them in a cold frame or greenhouse over the winter.

Always on the look out for 'free' plants, I discovered that the lowest shoots on our allotment rosemary had begun to root themselves into the ground. Cut off, potted up and nurtured over the summer they made healthy plants – and welcome gifts for other gardeners. (Ruth)

Sage

Once you've spent an hour relaxing at the allotment looking at the bees visiting sage flowers you'll never want to be without it. (Ruth)

You can grow sage for the allotment from seed, but it is much quicker and easier to pick up an inexpensive young plant from a nursery or bag a cutting from a friend. You will very soon have a handsome shrub and an all-year supply of leaves.

Ordinary sage has pretty blue flowers, but if you use a lot of sage in cooking and want consistent flavour you may prefer to grow a non-flowering variety such as the broad-leafed sage. Variegated sages are pretty, but not as flavoursome as the regular kind.

Sage needs little attention in the allotment and is reliably drought-resistant, though it will appreciate a mulch in spring before it starts back into growth (this will also help it produce plenty of foliage). Sage plants get straggly after a few years and will benefit from a good cut-back in autumn, after flowering. It also pays to renew sages now and again. Heeled cuttings, taken during the summer, will root relatively easily in a mixture of potting compost and sharp sand. Overwinter them in a cold frame or greenhouse, or in a cool room indoors.

Bay

With a bay on your plot you will have a handsome shrub and a constant supply of aromatic leaves. Be prepared, however, for a plant that outgrows your expectations, and survives against all odds.

> *A friend's father had a bay and he gave us a slip which we put in. When we came back to the same allotments 30 years later (though not on the same plot) it had grown into a huge tree. The people on that plot had tried to destroy it but with no success. It was one of our nicest allotment experiences. (Richard Harding)*

All you need for a bay is a sunny spot and secateurs to keep it under control. Small plants are much cheaper than large ones and will quickly establish themselves. To take cuttings in late summer, select lateral shoots and remove them with a 'heel'. Inserted into pots filled with equal parts of potting compost and sharp sand, and kept in a frost-free place for the subsequent winter, they should have rooted by spring. However, it may take another year, at least, for them to begin to grow strongly.

Thyme

If you are growing thyme for cooking as well as for its looks, best choice for the allotment is one of the upright sorts, rather than prostrate or creeping thyme. As well as the common thyme, look for plants or seeds of the lemon or silver queen thyme or the orange-scented 'Fragrantissimus'. Thymes look lovely edging a sunny allotment path, and it is worth having several so that you can harvest them freely all year.

Thymes will grow well from seed sown in spring, although they can be slow to get going and, because they are prone to damping off, need to be watered sparingly. Even when established they hate wet winters, so put them where they will get plenty of winter sun and where the soil is well drained.

If you want to enlarge your thyme collection with cuttings, take them in May or June and root them in a mixture of potting compost and sharp sand.

> *There is no accounting for thymes. Some winters they survive well, in others they give up the ghost. Experience proves that they do best in maximum sun. A few plants put in a shady place just didn't make it. (Ruth)*

Tarragon

Once they are well established, one or two good plants of tarragon will come up year after year to provide you with tasty aromatic leaves. But for the pure flavour you need to choose the French, not Russian, variety of this perennial. Buy young plants from a nursery and put them with your other permanent allotment herbs, ideally in a sunny spot with light, well-drained soil that has been well manured. Slugs can be a pest with tarragon.

To help protect tarragon from winter weather (it dislikes extremes of cold and wet) wait until spring to cut off all the previous year's growth. To keep plants vigorous, dig them up and divide them every two or three years. Do this in spring when they are beginning to grow well.

Lopping off tarragon flower heads once they appear and cutting back shoots with fading leaves stimulates a new growth of leaves and keeps tarragon going right up to the autumn. (Ruth)

Mint

Because it can be so invasive, the allotment is an excellent place to grow mint, but even there you will need to keep it in check. If you don't have a special area designated for herbs, a good place for mint is near the shed, in a spot that would otherwise be unculti-vated. Wherever you decide to put it, you can either take your chance on keeping mint confined by digging up and cutting back its spreading roots every autumn, or by making a 'corral' for the roots with one or more large biscuit tins with plenty of holes pierced in the base or, even better:

Big drainpipes are good for herbs like mint – to contain them. (Damien Grove)

Apart from spearmint there are other good mints to choose from, including hairy-leafed apple mint, lemon mint and eau-de-cologne mint whose foliage is a deep greenish purple. Even more unusual, and less rampant than their relatives (though more susceptible to frost), are ginger, orange and pineapple mints.

Marjoram (oregano)

Be careful when you decide to plant this vigorous perennial herb also known as oregano, from its scientific name, *Origanum*. Once established it can spread itself everywhere, though it makes a pretty edging and, when in flower, is a magnet for insects. As well as the common marjoram there are other forms, like pot marjoram, with golden leaf variegations. Less tolerant of cold and wet – and therefore less invasive – is sweet marjoram (*O. marjorana*), which also has extremely aromatic leaves. This is best grown as an annual.

All marjorams need a sunny spot and, ideally, well-drained soil. You can start from seeds or, more conveniently, from small plants. If you see the herb growing around the allotments, ask someone for a few rooted pieces, which they will almost certainly give you willingly.

To keep a good supply of leaves going it is helpful to cut back the flower shoots once they appear, though you may want to leave some plants uncut to attract bees and butterflies. If plants get too big you can simply dig them up in spring when they are beginning to make new growth, and divide them.

If you want to grow marjoram from seed, which is preferable for the sweet kind, then you need to start them indoors, in the warm, in early March, and harden them off before you plant them out. Sweet marjoram cuttings are also easy to strike.

An easy way to keep marjoram under control is to cut it well back as soon as it flowers. It will then make lots of new growth and more blooms, so you won't be depriving the bees. (Ruth)

Lemon balm

Lemon balm is a bit like horseradish, once you've got it you're never rid of it. (Ruth)

Unless you already have it growing on your plot, add lemon balm with care. The dark green aromatic, lemony leaves are lovely when they first appear but as they flower the plants soon become big and straggly. The plants quickly spread themselves, and the seeds are incredibly fertile, popping up as weeds all over the plot. It is easiest to keep under control if you cut it right back as soon as it comes into flower.

Lemon verbena

My favourite of all the herbs – just lovely. (Pat Cosgrove)

This lemon-scented herb with purple flowers is a totally different proposition from lemon balm but more problematic as it is a half hardy perennial which needs lots of sun and will not survive frost. One good way of keeping it going is to grow it in a pot that can be put in a frost-free spot in a greenhouse or even taken home over the winter.

Lovage

Two or three lovage plants will give you as many tasty leaves as you can deal with – and more. Because they will grow to at least 1.2 m (4 ft) in height, the best place for them is in a corner of the allotment or along the edge.

Three lovage plants grown from seed and put in the front of a plot in poor soil quickly outstripped us both in height – at their maximum they were probably nearly 1.8 m (6 ft) tall. They made leaves in profusion and came up again year after year. (Ruth)

Lovage seeds can be planted in pots in spring or autumn, then transplanted to their permanent positions. Taking off the flowers as they appear will give you more leaves. Although they are generally frost hardy, resist cutting them right back to ground level in autumn. A little growth left on will afford added protection. If plants get out of hand, dig them up and divide them in spring.

Chives and garlic chives

Both sorts of chives are simple to grow and pretty when they flower – 'regular' chives with purple heads, garlic chives with white ones. They make an attractive edging but are also useful in helping to deter pests like carrot fly, which may also influence where you put them.

Three good clumps of each sort will provide you with plenty of chives throughout the summer and well into the autumn. Garlic chives, which taste stronger, have flat – not rounded – leaves, and tend to form smaller clumps. You can grow both sorts from seed or plants. All will benefit from being dug up and divided into clumps of about a dozen shoots every three years or so, ideally in autumn.

If spores of rust are around, chives may be affected. Plenty of water and regular feeding will help make plants resistant, but there is no treatment.

When the first chives begin to come up in spring, dig up a few, pop them in a pot and put them in the kitchen. They quickly shoot up and by the time they are finished the 'main crop' is ready for picking. (Ruth)

Parsley

Who's in charge? It's a family joke with us that my parsley always grows well for, as the old rhyme goes, 'Where parsley grows faster, the mistress is master.' (Ruth)

The ubiquitous kitchen herb is a rewarding allotment grower, though you need to be patient as the seed is slow to germinate. All parsley is biennial, going to seed in its second year, so you need to plant it afresh every year to ensure consistent supplies.

Whether you choose plain or curly-leafed parsley seeds (such as the old-fashioned 'Moss Curled'), or some of each, they all need plenty of moisture and, ideally, a consistent temperature to germinate and grow well. An old trick is to pour boiling water on them after planting, to speed germination, but in fact this does not make a great deal of difference. They will always take two to four weeks to come through, even with the help of some heat.

Sowing seeds at home in pots or trays – in March for summer crops and July for winter ones – is a good way of getting allotment parsley going, though their roots elongate very quickly and they do not respond well to potting on. Once planted out – leave about 30 cm (1 ft) between plants – continue to water them well and keep them fed.

Being a relative of the carrot, parsley is prone to attack by carrot root fly, though growing chives, garlic or onions alongside will help deter these pests.

Basil

No summer allotment should be without basil. Because it will only thrive when well and truly warm, it is best not to start it off too early. May is fine for seed planting outdoors, and even then your basil will appreciate being germinated under fleece or a cloche. For a harvest that goes on right until autumn make one or maybe even two more sowings.

When the seedlings are big enough to handle, either thin them out and replant the thinnings nearby, or transplant all your seedlings to a permanent spot. If the weather is cool they will appreciate continued cover until they are growing really well and by July or August you should have plenty of leaves to harvest.

Begin by taking leaves from near plant bases, then as soon as the plants look if as they are about to flower, pinch these out and use the tips. I've found that this prolongs their life and encourages them to make plenty of side shoots. (Ruth)

As well as ordinary sweet basil there are several other kinds that are both decorative and tasty, including deep purple or 'royal' basil, lemon basil, Neapolitan or lettuce-leafed basil with large, frilly leaves and the small-leafed bush basil.

Chervil

Although technically a biennial, chervil is best grown as an annual. This hardy herb has a superbly delicate flavour reminiscent of celery. For a continuous crop make two or three sowings throughout the summer, beginning in March, or when the soil has warmed up; early sowings will benefit from the protection of fleece or a cloche. The last sowing can be in September for winter leaves. Again, protection will help keep these going well.

Once seeds have germinated, you can thin plants to about 23 cm (9 in) apart. They do not respond well to being transplanted, but you can use the thinnings right away. Chervil likes drainage and partial shade rather than continuous blasts of full sun which will make it run quickly to seed.

Our first efforts with chervil were singularly poor. The leaves turned red, then brown which, we discovered, was because they were lacking in minerals. Having given up on it for a few years we tried again in Dorset soil – the chervil loves it. (Ruth)

Coriander

Like rocket, coriander – also called cilantro or Chinese parsley – is quick to grow and quick to run to seed, but well worth its place in the allotment for its aromatic leaves and spicy seeds. Sow seeds where you want them to mature.

When buying coriander seeds, check whether they are intended primarily for producing leaves (these may be called leaf coriander) or for seeds (often marketed as Moroccan coriander). Coriander needs sowing out late, to avoid young plants being frosted, and in succession up to early September if you want to have leaves for picking well into autumn, though it does best in weather that is not too hot and dry. Plenty of water will help prevent plants bolting too quickly, as will a partly shaded place on the plot and regular picking of the leaves.

> *When the seeds turn brown I pick off coriander stems and hang them upside down to dry, then strip off the seeds and keep them in an airtight container over the winter. (Ruth)*

Dill

This easy-to-grow annual with its aniseed flavour needs an open, sunny site and enough warmth – a night-time temperature of 7ºC (45ºF) or above – to germinate successfully. As with herbs such as coriander it pays to plant dill little and often for a plentiful supply of leaves all summer.

Dill dislikes being transplanted, so is best sown where it will stay, and thinned out a little – just use the young leaves. Plenty of water and an occasional feed is all it needs. When plants flower you can pick these whole to flavour pickles or leave them to go to seed, then pick and dry the heads and save the seeds for cooking and planting.

Fennel

Unlike Florence fennel, which is grown as a vegetable (see p. 126), ordinary or common fennel is a useful allotment herb. The number and type of plants you grow will depend on whether you are planning to harvest the seeds as well as the leaves. For seeds you may want to choose the attractive bronze-leafed fennel rather than the soft green type.

Fennel grows easily from seed sown in spring; it can be started in pots and seedlings transplanted, or begun in its permanent position and thinned out to about 23 cm (9 in). If you are not going to harvest the seeds, cutting the flower heads down to their base will increase foliage production. For seeds, wait until the heads are just turning brown before snipping them off for drying. When plants die back in autumn, mulch them well. They benefit – in both vigour and flavour – from being divided every three or four years.

One particularly wet spring and summer the fennel grew more than 2 metres (6 ft) high, though it needed staking to prevent it from being blown down by the wind. A sunny autumn ripened the seeds up brilliantly. (Ruth)

Borage

With leaves that have a cucumber flavour (the essential flavouring for Pimm's and other punches), borage has the bonus of bright blue flowers. Borage is a hardy annual easy to grow from seed and will self-sow in the same spot for years on end. Bees love it, too.

Horseradish

Even under an apple tree it grew and spread everywhere, even though the roots were puny. (Ruth)

While it is great to have your own supplies of fresh horseradish, think twice before you plant it. Vigorous and invasive, and tolerant of the worst soil, horseradish can take over a large area in no time and is almost impossible to eradicate except with weedkiller. If an allotment neighbour has horseradish you may be able to beg or borrow roots as you need them rather than growing it yourself.

The best way of cultivating – and confining – horseradish is to grow it in pieces of drainpipe about 2 ft (60 cm) long pushed into the ground and filled with a compost and soil mixture. In March a piece of root, ideally 6 to 12 in (15 to 30 cm) long can then be planted into each container and, as they mature, can be used as you need them. Lift the crop in early winter and try to get rid of every bit of root.

ALLOTMENT FLOWERS

I grow flowers – I just put them in and see what happens. I don't bother with vegetables. I just like looking at them. (Phyllis De Sousa)

The allotment is a wonderful place to grow flowers. They are ideal for cutting and arranging and can often help the health of allotment vegetables by deterring pests and diseases and encouraging pest predators. And many allotment favourites, such as sweet peas and gladioli, are flowers that are hard to fit into border schemes.

I grew things I didn't have room for at home. I grew dahlias, big alliums and dianthus. (Pat Bence)

However, not everyone agrees that flowers should be the centrepiece of an allotment.

When we first came and started making flower beds the lady next door said, 'You don't put your flowers like that, you put them on the edge.' But I just put them where I wanted. (Brendan Coffrey)

The old men were frightfully dismissive because Jane liked to grow cornflowers, marigolds and such. But things are a bit different now. (Richard Harding)

Edible flowers

Apart from herb flowers (borage, dill, fennel, chive and coriander flowers are all edible), you may want to grow some courgettes specifically for their tasty blooms (see p. 145). Two other good edible flowers to grow for salads are nasturtiums and marigolds.

NASTURTIUMS

Vibrant nasturtiums are guaranteed to brighten any plot. Just sow the seeds in April and wait for them to mature. They look great on the top of a compost heap and set between tomato plants will help to ward off whitefly. If you leave them to self-seed they will come back every year. Look out for caterpillars, which can quickly devastate entire plants.

One day the leaves of our nasturtiums looked vibrant and healthy, on the next visit they had been virtually devoured. The culprits were the unmistakable cabbage white butterfly caterpillars. A good dousing with a hose got rid of most of them and the plants quickly recovered. (Ruth)

MARIGOLDS

The marigolds to grow for edible petals are pot marigolds (*Calendula officinalis*). These hardy annuals, with their orange or yellow daisy-like flowers are simple to grow from seed and will thrive in any sunny position. You can wait until late spring and sow seed direct into the plot or begin them indoors in early spring. Deadhead them regularly and you will have flowers for weeks on end. If you plant them near your asparagus they are reputed to help deter attacks by asparagus beetles.

Sweet peas

Having them at the allotment, up canes put behind the shed and alongside the fence, is ideal. I've tried them in pots, but this is much better. Best of all is to have them out in the plot like runner beans. (Ruth)

Grow sweet peas for their gorgeous scent. You can grow them in rows, using a double row of canes as you would for runner beans, up wigwams, or against a netting fence, depending on the room you have, but it will pay to tie string around and between the canes to make horizontal supports.

Sweet pea seeds can be slow to germinate, and do well if you soak them in water overnight or place them between two pieces of damp kitchen paper.

I've chitted them, soaked them and put them straight in – I don't think it makes much difference. If I soak them I discard any that float. (Pat Cosgrove)

The sweet pea experts sow their seeds in November – with six or seven in a 13-cm (5-in) pot – keeping them in a cold frame or sheltered outdoor spot (and if necessary covered with polythene or fleece) then planting them out in March. And there are other ways of nurturing them:

I've grown them in tubes, toilet rolls – all different ways – I just love sweet peas. (Pat Cosgrove)

One of the tricks of success is to avoid overwatering them during this period. And as with all plants, patience is required:

Everyone said wait for them and they will come – and they did. I just love looking at them. (Phyllis De Sousa)

It is also fine to sow seed in the same way, or direct into the ground, in March. Whichever method you choose, pinch out the tops of the plants once they have four or five leaves. That way you will get plenty of strong flower-bearing side shoots.

I dig a 2-foot trench – or as deep as I can until I hit the chalk. The roots then go right down to get the moisture, especially in dry weather. (David Downton)

For really show-stopping sweet peas, as you train each plant up a cane, tie it in at regular intervals and pinch out all the side shoots, pinch out the tendrils and remove any flowers as they develop. When each plant gets to the top of the cane, untie it, lay half of each stem along the ground and train the other half up a cane a little farther along the row. With plenty of food and water, long-stemmed heads, each with five or six flowers, should be produced.

Water and feed sweet peas well and keep off weeds and pests. Keep picking them regularly to extend the flowering season and deadhead them regularly.

I use scissors to snip over the plants every few days, removing any miniature seed pods that are forming. (Ruth)

There are dozens of varieties to choose from but for superior scents, choose the old-fashioned sweet pea varieties like 'Old Fashioned Scented Mixed' and 'Old Spice Mixed'.

Sweet pea flowers are attractive to pollen beetles, which lodge inside the enclosed keel petals. An old-fashioned way of getting rid of them is to put cut flowers in a yellow bucket. The beetles will fly out, attracted by the colour.

Dahlias

Tender, thirsty and showy, dahlias flourish on most allotment sites and are excellent for cutting and for show. They also attract useful pollinators. The cultivation season begins in mid March, when you need to start setting stored or newly bought tubers in potting compost, cutting large bunches of tubers into smaller sections to increase your stock. Keep them in a light, frost-free place and give them plenty of water until they are well grown (you may need to transfer them to larger pots if they get too big). By late May they will be ready to plant out.

You can also take cuttings from tubers sprouted in late winter in multi-purpose compost (leave just the stems showing). When you take the cuttings, leave a small sliver of the parent tuber on the end. Remove the lower leaves, dip in hormone rooting powder and place in a pot and water them. If you enclose the pot in a plastic bag the cuttings will root in about three weeks. They can then be potted on singly.

You need to take cuttings of them in the spring. With tubers you don't get such good plants. (Doug Chainey)

Plant dahlias at a depth of about 15 cm (6 in), with the old stems pointing upwards. To help water retention, it pays to plant dahlias in ground that has been thoroughly composted, and to mulch them well, especially if you are not able to water them every day in dry spells. You also need to protect plants, but especially young ones, from slugs and snails, which relish their juicy foliage. Earwigs also love the flowers, where they will hide. To trap them, try putting a pot filled with straw upside down on the top of a cane among plants. Check it every day and empty out the earwigs inside.

To catch earwigs, put empty 12-bore cartridge cases on top of canes beside your dahlias and every morning take them off, put your finger inside and crush them. We call these 'battle twigs'. (Mike Wiffen)

Large plants will also need staking to prevent them being broken by the wind. They need deadheading regularly.

There are thousands of dahlias to choose from, but some easy, showy ones include:

- 'Jomanda' – long, straight stems and ball-shaped flowers in a beautiful burnt orange;
- 'Marlene Joy' – spiky flowers with pink-tipped white petals;
- 'Moor Place' – a handsome pompom variety with purple blooms;
- 'Zorro' – giant, decorative purplish-red flowers;
- 'Baret Joy' – white, semi-cactus type;
- 'Raiser's Pride' – medium cactus, salmon pink flowers.

I have dahlias that come back year after year – I just leave them. (Phyllis De Sousa)

In mild winters, dahlia tubers may survive without being lifted, but are best dug up and removed from the plot once their foliage has died down or been killed by frost. Tubers are disease-prone and need to be kept carefully; allow them to dry out upside down, so that moisture can drain from the stem remnants. And don't forget to label them.

Canker and other fungal diseases such as grey mould (botrytis) are the major threats to dahlia tubers over the winter. Powdered sulphur is among the oldest and most effective deterrents. After lifting, sprinkle them liberally with sulphur and place them right way up in straw-filled boxes. Alternatively dip the dried tubers in a proprietary fungicide, dry them again and pack them with their tops (crowns) exposed in peat or sand.

Asters

More correctly called China asters, these tender, daisy-like flowers of the genus *Callistephus* feature in show schedules and on many allotments throughout the country. These annuals come in almost every shade of blue, red and white and in single, double and semi-double forms.

Asters have done well for me. I brought on the seed in my little plastic greenhouse then pricked them out. (Robin Barrett)

For the best asters, sow seed in early spring and keep plants under glass or some other protection, or sow seed direct into the allotment in late spring. They need to be hardened off before being planted out and prefer sun, shelter from wind and good drainage. If you want to grow asters for show, select the taller, long-stemmed varieties and stake them if need be. Nipping out the side buds will give you bigger, more stunning blooms.

As well as the usual slugs, the main problems with asters are aphids and a disease called callistephus wilt caused by the fusarium fungus. To prevent this infection, which will make plants collapse and die, be sure not to overwater them, especially when young, and remove all deadheads as soon as the flowers have faded. To prevent build-up of fungal spores in the soil, rotate the positions of your asters, as for vegetables. As an extra insurance, look out for seed advertised as wilt resistant.

I had loads of slugs – they got the lot – so now I put them in pots. (Pat Cosgrove)

Packets of mixed seeds will give you a range of flower colours. The most popular ones are:

- 'Duchess Mix' – large chrysanthemum-like flowers, plants of intermediate size;
- 'Milady Mixed' – dwarf plants; large flowers with incurved petals;
- 'Teisa Stars Mix' – double flowers with long, quilled petals;
- 'Ostrich Plume Mix' – large, feathery blooms.

Zinnias

I grow them from seed and prick them out at the allotment. They do well there. (Robin Barrett)

Zinnias are favourites of flower arrangers and if not grown from seed can be brought on as young plants. For early displays you can begin seed in the warmth in April; they will germinate well outdoors later in spring. They like plenty of moisture and full sun, and come in a range of colours from deep crimson to white and even pale green, and in singles and doubles.

Gladioli

Gladioli make first-rate allotment flowers, are easy to grow and come in a huge variety of colours and in various shapes, including the pretty butterfly hybrids.

The corms came from an end of clearance sale and were all half price – they were even starting to sprout in the packets. They came out very well. I just stuck them in and left them. I put them by the fence so I could have tied them to it if they'd gone over. (Robin Barrett)

If you plant corms in three or four batches between mid March and mid April you should have flowers to cut all summer. For really early blooms you can sprout the corms in a light, warm spot from mid February, before planting them about 10 cm (4 in) deep in well-manured soil (put them a little deeper if your plot is very windy) and in rows about 30 cm (1 ft) apart. Putting a little sand in each planting hole will help with drainage on heavier soils. Just keep the slugs and snails off, and give them plenty of water. Should they need extra protection from the wind, insert a stick on the side of each plant facing the prevailing wind and simply tie in the base.

I dug a channel and filled it with rough sand – I've had some beauties. I'm not going to save the corms – it's said they all throw back to pink. (Mike Wiffen)

Tender gladioli need lifting and storing over the winter if you choose to save them. After the first winter frosts dig up the corms, trim the tops and put them upside down in a shallow box or tray in a dark, airy place. Be sure to label them. In spring, peel off any shrivelled tissue and break off any small corms (cormlets) before replanting. The cormlets can be planted, but will not usually flower until their second year.

Roses

On a summer evening it is a real pleasure to be able to bring home a bunch of roses from the allotment. (Ruth)

Roses tolerate most soils – though are especially fond of clay – and also periods of drought, which means that they will survive well without a lot of attention.

For best value, buy bare-rooted roses of your choice by mail order. Most companies deliver between October and March so that plants can be set out while they are still dormant. As long as the roots are kept moist and frost free, they can be stored in their packaging until you are ready to plant them out and until the ground is workable and reasonably dry. In any event, soaking the roots in a bucket of water for an hour before planting is always a good idea.

Before planting, make up a mixture of one part soil, one part peat, and add two handfuls of bone meal. Then dig a hole large enough to spread the roots out evenly and use your enriched mixture to cover them. Firm this in by treading around the plant. Scatter some manure or mushroom compost around each plant and cover it with a loose layer of soil. If the rose has been grafted, which is most likely, the bud union should be just a little below the soil surface.

If you buy container-grown roses, they are also best planted over the winter and, in a dry spell, kept well watered for their first two or three weeks. Your aim with these should be to disturb them as little as possible. Dig a hole just large enough for the size of the container then ease the plant free and fit it into the hole. Then follow the guidelines above.

As your roses bloom, pick them regularly and remove any deadheads to keep them flowering. Leave pruning until spring, then use sharp, clean secateurs to cut out any dead wood and spindly shoots. On healthy branches, make sloping cuts, beginning on the side farthest from the bud or eye and slanting towards it, finishing just above the eye. Then feed well with a top dressing of compost.

If you have inherited old roses on your plot, cut away half the shoots to the base of the plant one year, then the other half the second year. Given a mulch of compost in spring, you will be amazed how quickly old roses will recover.

I think there is a lot of bunk talked about rose pruning. I say prune them to the shape you want. They will take any amount of cutting back. (Mike Cosgrove)

To get best value from allotment roses, good choices are those that repeat flower well into the autumn.

From the many dozens of varieties available, these are some good ones. Any of the climbers/ramblers would look well over an allotment shed or against a fence or other boundary.

Ramblers

'Ballerina'	Pink
'Gertrude Jekyll'	Dark pink
Rosa x Micrugosa	Pale pink
'Fountain'	Red
'Iceberg'	White

Climbers

'Aloha'	Pink
'Golden Showers'	Yellow
Rosa filipes 'Kiftsgate'	White, many hips
'Handel'	Creamy white, edged in cherry red
'Madame Alfred Carrière'	White, double blooms, blush-tinted

When we moved allotments we would have been sad to lose the prolific pink roses we had inherited. Although it was August – not the perfect month for cuttings – we took a dozen anyway and potted them up. Several rooted well and we had roses every year thereafter. (Ruth)

Like garden roses, allotment plants are prey to the fungal infection black spot and to aphid infestation. For black spot you need to start treatment in early spring or choose resistant types. Treat aphids (greenfly) as you would your vegetables.

I've become more and more converted towards species roses – I get frustrated with the black spot. So many hybrid teas are susceptible to the black spot. Before the Clean Air Act I didn't have any black spot in sight. With species – like rugosa roses – you don't get any black spot at all. (Mike Cosgrove)

Sunflowers

Get them in early, they are great for the bees. (Sue Bryant)

Ideal for children to grow and measure on the allotment, sunflowers are great for cutting and attract bees and butterflies too. You can also use the seeds to provide food for birds as well as harvesting them for your own enjoyment.

For tall plants that will reach 1 to 2 m (3 to 6 ft) and edible seeds, choose a variety such as 'Mammoth' or 'Giant Yellow'; on a very windy plot you might prefer a shorter one such as 'Teddy Bear'. Many suppliers also sell packets of mixed seeds marketed under names such as 'Lucky Dip' that will give you lots of different shapes and sizes and multi colours.

Sunflower seeds can be sown under cover in March or April and planted out after frost risk is over, or put straight into the ground in May or early June. Place or thin them to about 60 cm (2 ft) apart. Choose the sunniest spot available and be sure to protect them well from slugs and snails. Rabbits will also devour them. As they shoot up you may need to stake them, as even heavy rain can make them collapse.

French marigolds

Whether you grow them from seed or buy them as young plants from the nursery, French marigolds are tender annuals that add colour to the allotment right through the season and well into autumn as long as you deadhead them regularly. Not just pretty, they can be useful too, helping to keep whitefly and other insect pests off crops such as tomatoes, both outdoors and in the greenhouse.

I've always grown French marigolds on either side of my tomatoes and they just flower right up until November, so there's always some colour. (Maureen Nightingale)

CHAPTER 5

GROWING FRUIT

Fruit on the allotment is great, as long as you can prevent the birds eating it before you do and – if you have tall fruit trees – you are able to harvest your crop. Fruit does take up a considerable amount of room, but you can save space by growing crops such as blackberries on wires along the allotment edge. Before planting fruit trees you may need to check what is allowed on your site.

SOFT FRUIT

Arguably the best of all, soft fruits are easy to grow as long as they are well fed and do not have to compete with a lot of weeds. Get rid of as many perennial weeds as possible before you plant soft fruit of any kind and weed them carefully. Plenty of manure or compost added before planting, and annual mulching, will feed them and improve water retention. For protection, netting will keep off the birds (see p. 80), which go most for the early crops – by the time the later ones are ready the birds seem to have eaten their fill.

Strawberries

There is nothing quite like the taste of allotment-grown strawberries eaten straight from the plant, but they need some back-breaking attention, and plenty of protection from slugs and birds if they are to yield a worthwhile crop. By choosing different varieties (three if you have the space) you can extend the season as much as possible and avoid massive gluts.

Maximum soil fertility and good water retention will help you get good strawberry crops, so dig in plenty of manure and get rid of as many perennial weeds as possible, or compost before you plant. Some people favour laying down weed-suppressing membrane (also available as individual 'mats') and planting strawberries through holes made in it. The newest sorts are coated with aluminium foil, which reflects both light and warmth onto the crop. Although they don't look very beautiful they have the added advantage of keeping slugs at bay.

If you inherit a strawberry bed with your plot, wait a year to see what it produces. We discovered that the strawberry bed left to us on one plot was so infested with convolvulus that we dug the whole lot up, sorted out the good plants and moved them to a better patch of ground. (Ruth)

You can buy plants from good nurseries or market stalls, but if you want specific varieties you may need to order them. Some good choices are 'Mae' for earlies, 'Cambridge Favourite' and 'Royal Sovereign' for mid season and 'Florence' for late. 'Flamenco', a perpetual or 'everbearer', produces fruit both early and late.

Ideally, set plants into the ground in autumn, while the ground is still warm, about 45 cm (18 in) apart, though aim to put perpetuals in during late summer.

In late spring, as soon as flowers are beginning to fade, strawberries can be 'strawed'. Even if you've had plenty of rain they should be watered well at this point, and the ground treated with slug pellets if you wish. You can then tuck straw under each plant. In wet weather, grey mould can ruin fruit before you get to pick it.

Alternatively you can avoid a lot of problems by raising plants above ground:

I grow strawberries in growbags on a scaffold plank. I put about four in a bag. It keeps off slugs and snails. You have to water them a bit more often, though. (Doug Chainey)

However you grow them, the best way to keep plants vigorous is to replace them every two or three years with new ones raised from the copious runners which appear in late summer.

These can be pegged into the soil until established, then moved to the position you want. To keep established plants vigorous, and to prevent the patch getting crowded out with new plants, snip off all the runners you don't need. In a fine autumn you may even get a bonus:

> Strawberries [in September] have just started to come again. A treat. (Maureen Nightingale)

After fruiting, remove the straw and dig it into the ground or put it on the compost heap. Then perk up the soil by forking in some compost around the plants. If you wish you can add about 15 g (½ oz) of sulphate of potash per bucketful.

Raspberries

Allotment raspberries, although they take up considerable space, are a rewarding crop and, if grown from healthy plants, remarkably free of trouble from pests and diseases.

> By mixing summer and autumn types we eat fresh raspberries almost every day from late June to October or even November. We grow them at one end of our plot so they form a kind of 'hedge'. (Ruth)

> I have about six varieties – the autumn varieties do very well. (Edward Probert)

Because they are shallow rooted all raspberries crave well-manured soil and minimal competition from perennial weeds. They also like plenty of sun and, if possible, to be sheltered from the wind. The summer sorts, especially, need to be provided with supports to prevent roots from rocking and stems from snapping. If you have just a few plants you can use a series of canes, but a whole row is best supported with a line of posts between which are strung a couple of wires at different heights, the top one at about 1.7 m (5 ft). As shoots grow, tie them in with plastic ties or strong string.

The best way to begin with all raspberries is with young plants put into the ground in November or March in a manured trench about 7.5 cm (3 in) deep, and about 45 cm (18 in) apart. After planting, cut the canes to about 5 cm (2 in) above soil level to discourage weak, twiggy growth and encourage good root systems.

The treatment that raspberries need then depends on when they fruit. This is because summer raspberries such as 'Glen Moy' and 'Glen Cava' fruit on old wood, made the previous year, while autumn raspberries like 'Autumn Bliss' and the yellow 'Fall Gold' fruit on the current year's growth.

SUMMER RASPBERRIES

To get strong, healthy plants, don't let summer raspberries fruit in their first year. When shoots come into flower, cut the tops off them before they have a chance to fruit. In subsequent years, cut back canes that have fruited to a few inches from the ground in the autumn and prune any straggly tops from new canes.

AUTUMN RASPBERRIES

Once these have fruited, leave the canes in place until early spring, then cut them all back to ground level. Keep the sturdiest canes – they make good pea sticks.

Every spring, take out any weeds as they appear and give your raspberries a good mulch. This will help water retention, as well as helping to provide protection against disease. You can use manure, bark or other woody debris, which will feed them as well, ideally re-creating the acid conditions of the woodlands in which they grow in the wild.

Because healthy plants will spread rapidly you may find new plants sprouting all over the place in spring. Dig up those you don't want before your patch gets overcrowded. If you want to renew old plants (they should last up to a decade), pot up these spares and grow them on so that you can make replacements in the autumn.

You plant one stem and I swear that 20 come up. I think I should have had some fencing or something to prop them up. (Robin Barrett)

Very wet summers can bring on the fungal diseases spur blight, which makes shoots (spurs) die back, and cane blight, which makes canes die back and snap off at ground level. In both cases, diseased plants need to be dug up and burnt or safely disposed of. Raspberry beetles can also lay their eggs on raspberry flowers. The brown grubs that hatch burrow their way into the centre of the fruit and distort them. Keep a watch out for the beetles and dispose of them. Tapping the heads of the canes will make them drop off – as they do so you can collect them in a bucket, which makes them easy to kill.

Gooseberries

I love gooseberries and you can't get them in the shops. (Pat Bence)

If gooseberries are a fruit you favour, make room for at least one bush on your allotment and you will not be disappointed. When choosing new plants – they are best bought two or three years old – it may pay to select varieties with good mildew resistance such as the high-yielding 'Invicta' and the lovely red-fruited dessert gooseberry 'Pax'. More susceptible – but worth trying – are 'Whinham's Industry' and 'Keepsake'. To allow for vigorous growth, which will also discourage mildew, be sure to leave at least 1.5 m (5 ft) between bushes. 'Captivator' has red fruit and is nearly thornless.

I get potash from the trading post and give them a good feed before and after I've picked them. (Mike Wiffen)

As well as mildew, which in the last resort can be treated with sulphur (test spray a single shoot to check this will not scorch the plant), the other common problem with goose-berries is the gooseberry sawfly, whose caterpillars can quickly strip a plant of its leaves. If you act in time, removing the offenders by hand is the best solution to this problem, though you can use derris if you wish.

Pruning will keep gooseberries healthy and fruiting well. Your aim should be to keep plants nice and open. In winter (and well before March), cut back current season's shoots to about half their length, and cut away any branches that are crossing.

Having been ripped to pieces in the past I always make sure I'm wearing long sleeves, thick gloves and even a hat when I'm pruning gooseberries and weeding underneath them. (Ruth)

If you want more plants, they grow very readily from cuttings.

Blackcurrants

The distinctive smell of blackcurrants is one of the pleasures of the allotment. As with gooseberries the latest cultivars of blackcurrants are bred to be resistant to mildew and you can expect heavy crops year after year from reliable varieties such as 'Ben Connan' and 'Ben Sarek'.

Because blackcurrants freeze so well it is worth growing several bushes if you have room. They are also easy to propagate from cuttings, so you can always expand your collection later on. Plant out bushes in the autumn or winter, allowing about 1.75 m (6 ft) between each, into soil that has been thoroughly composted. To strengthen young bushes, cut them down to about 2.5 cm (1 in) after planting. It will be worth sacrificing the first year's crop.

My son has a pigeon loft and throws the water he's used for cleaning them out onto his blackcurrants. They are huge. (Mike Wiffen)

Routine tasks with blackcurrants are keeping them well mulched in both spring and autumn and keeping them pruned, cutting out old wood so as to keep the centre of each bush open and uncrowded. Because blackcurrants fruit on new wood, this is best done in early autumn. If you decide to protect bushes with netting individually, remember to allow room for the bush to grow – it is infuriating to have branches pushing through the netting – and make sure any netting you use is easy to take off when you want to pick the fruit.

I've watched them. Given the choice between raspberries, strawberries and black-currants, birds go straight for the blackcurrants. (Ruth)

The one pest you don't want is the blackcurrant big bud mite, which makes the buds swell, and even drop off. You can pick these off and burn them as they appear, but because there is no effective pesticide the only solution is to dig up and burn heavily infested plants. When you replant, look for the mite-resistant cultivar 'Ben Hope'.

To take blackcurrant cuttings, in October, snip off pieces of the current year's growth, trim off the soft tip of each one just above a bud and place the cuttings in a small trench in a corner of the plot. Within a year they should be well rooted and ready to transplant.

Red and white currants

Just one redcurrant bush will give you plenty of fruit for sauces and jellies and to freeze for dishes like summer pudding. For heaviest crops, 'Rovada' is a recommended variety. If you also like white currants, which are grown in the same way, 'Blanka' is a good choice.

Cultivation of these fruit is generally as for blackcurrants. However, they need pruning differently because they fruit on old, not new wood. For this reason pruning is best done in February, making cuts back to strong buds and shortening each branch by about half. As the bushes mature, cut out old wood from the centre if it is making the bush congested.

Once I learned about redcurrants fruiting on old wood it all made sense. (Ruth)

Gall bud mites may attack redcurrants as well as black, and redcurrants are also susceptible to coral spot, a fungus characterized by red cushion-like lumps on the wood of the plant. Any shoots that show such disease should be cut out and destroyed, ideally by burning.

Blackberries

Blackberries seem to thrive on allotments and often grow wild around allotment edges and paths for all to pick and enjoy.

Because they grow so vigorously, think carefully about where you are going to put allotment blackberries. If you have fencing around your perimeter, additional supports plus horizontal wires will allow you to train them relatively easily and keep them neat. A couple of varieties fruiting at different times, such as the early, spine-free 'Helen' and the later 'Black Butte' with huge, juicy berries, are both good choices. For space saving, try the upright 'Loch Tay'. To avoid problems later, put supports in place before you begin.

Plant out cultivated types at any time from November to March. Apart from an annual mulch, and pruning of fruited stems to ground level, they need very little care.

We stop blackberries from spreading too much by trying to prevent wayward stems from bending over and touching the ground and either tying them in or cutting them back. If you leave them they'll root into new plants in a matter of weeks – though this is useful if you want to propagate them. (Ruth)

Hybrid fruit

You can grow loganberries, boysenberries and tayberries in the same way as blackberries, though all need plenty of space. All yield well in a sunny spot, although loganberries are not fond of chalk. For ease of handling both branches and fruit, look for the latest thornless varieties.

> *Loganberries are lovely – they have a sweetness and a sharpness all together. (Maureen Nightingale)*

You may even be lucky enough to find a hybrid of your own.

> *The hybrids I grow are awkwardly productive. I've got one of my own discovery – a kind of tayberry that was growing in our last garden. It must be an accidental cross spread by birds. I grew it on and have done that twice more. It has a tayberry-like fruit and is slightly smaller. The growth pattern is better – it shoots only from the crown. It's quite flexible and easily trained and its fruit season is quite extensive. (Edward Probert)*

Cape gooseberries (physalis)

Expensive to buy, these stunning-looking fruits are extremely easy to grow in a sunny place as long as you can keep them from being eaten by slugs, snails and rabbits and you can give them lots of water and sunshine.

Cape gooseberry seeds need to be germinated in the warmth – ideally under glass at 18–21ºC (65–70ºF) and planted out in May or June about 60 cm (2 ft) apart. 'Regular' species plants will grow up to 2 m (6 ft) but there are also good dwarf varieties such as 'Little Lantern', which are generally sturdier.

Once flowers have been germinated and fruits are beginning to form, keep the plants fed with a general fertilizer (tomato fertilizer is fine). They are ready to eat when they have turned orange and the husks have turned papery.

> *In exchange for some lettuce seedlings our neighbour gave us some cape gooseberry plants to try. They did really well and tasted delicious. (Ruth)*

Blueberries

Unless you have extremely acid soil you'll only be able to grow blueberries in big pots or a raised bed, or in a confined area filled with ericaceous compost. But there are other ways of getting the medium you need.

I put in some grass compost that had gone completely fluid. Everyone says you can't grow them here but I've had a great crop and they look beautiful in autumn – glowing with lovely reds and oranges. (Vicky Scott)

If you choose pots, select those that will withstand frost – blueberries will not fruit unless exposed to winter cold. Plant young bushes in winter, from November to March, and add a mulch of sawdust or wood shreddings.

Apart from needing a yearly feed in spring they need little attention but will appreciate a twice-yearly addition of sulphate of iron to keep the acidity high. Prune off any low branches that touch the soil and, annually, any dead wood.

The fruit is borne on the tips of the previous season's growth, but because they fruit late in the year you need to prune in winter to encourage this, taking back about a third of the branches on a mature bush. Birds love them, so they definitely need netting. They also need to be kept moist.

Tea bags make an excellent mulch for blueberry plants and help prevent early drop caused by drought in dry spells. (Tim Callard)

Rhubarb

Just one good rhubarb crown will give you more than enough to feed a family, and with a bit of ingenuity you can have rhubarb on your table really early. An allotment corner is a good place for rhubarb, as long as it has enough room to expand – and you may well find you already have some.

Whenever you take on a plot you always inherit rhubarb in one corner. Sometimes it's OK, sometimes not. (Robin Barrett)

Both autumn and early spring – as long as the ground is not frozen – are good times for planting rhubarb crowns and, true to their reputation, they thrive on soil enriched with plenty of organic matter. Don't plant the crowns too deeply; the new shoots should be above the surface of the ground.

Never pick rhubarb after mid July – it damages the crowns. (Tim Callard)

For an extra early crop, cover the crown with straw or bracken over the winter, then in late January or early February put an upturned bucket, old drainpipe or a proper rhubarb forcer over the plant to encourage news shoots. 'Timperley Early' is an ideal variety. Irresistible for its name alone, 'Red Champagne' will come later.

Keep your rhubarb well watered and mulched. Pull or cut out any flowers as soon as they appear, to prevent weakening plants.

TREE FRUIT

Fruit trees can do well on an allotment if you have the space – and as long as trees are allowed. But there are snags, not least because picking and pruning a large tree can be difficult. Also trees create shade, and will sap a lot of water from the surrounding soil. If you are lucky enough to inherit an existing tree in good condition it is worth working to keep it that way. Or you may want to try reviving existing but neglected trees rather than have them cut down or taken out.

Apples

An apple tree or two can add greatly to a plot, and you may acquire trees with your allotment.

On our Highgate plot we inherited two apple trees which, though they desperately needed pruning, didn't look in too bad a condition. Later we discovered that they had been planted many years before as ungrafted plants grown from pips. They were never wonderful but better than no fruit at all. (Ruth)

OLD TREES

Before you decide to try renovating an old tree, wait and see whether it is healthy enough to produce any fruit. To find out what variety it is, try matching it with illustrations in books or on websites, or look out for 'apple days' at your local nursery. In winter, when a decent tree is dormant, begin by cutting out as much dead wood as possible and any branches that cross each other so that you get a nice, open centre. If the branches are too thick to respond to loppers they will need to be sawn through, for which you will almost certainly need a tall ladder (and probably someone to hold it for you).

> *Our apple pruning always attracted attention. Because trees were right by the path, we received, as we worked, different pruning advice from virtually every passer-by. There was never any shortage of unsolicited help on offer. (Ruth)*

If your apple is a 'bush' type (which will not produce fruit buds at the tips of the branches) you will need to cut back excess growth from the top of the tree if you can. If branches are long and smooth, reduce the tops of these by about a third. If it is a spur-producing apple (you'll recognize it by the short, rather knobbly side shoots that grow from the branches) cut back both the branch tops and any large side shoots. Should you be lucky enough to inherit a 'Bramley' or 'Worcester Pearmain', both of which produce fruit near the tips of their branches, thin out the tree centre. If you need to, just take the tops of branch leaders to a good-looking bud but avoid lopping off tips of the lateral shoots.

Once the tree is in good shape, keep it that way by pruning every winter. There is no need to paint over the cut ends of the branches, but a pruned tree will appreciate some feeding. Rather than spreading compost around the base of the trunk, dig a series of holes about 23 cm (9 in) deep, fill them with manure and water them in well. The same goes for established trees you've planted yourself.

NEW TREES

Starting from scratch, you first of all need to decide whether you need two or even three trees or whether just one will do. Look around and see how neighbours' trees are doing. Two pollinators will be essential unless your apples are self-fertile. A Bramley will need at least two other varieties as pollinators. What's essential is to know which pollinating group (A, B, or C) the apple of your choice belongs to. To get fruit you need matches from the same group.

The advantage of beginning with young trees is that as well as giving you the choice of your favourite varieties, you should be assured of healthy stock. Also you can keep trees in shape by pruning a little each year. A nicely compact variety will help avoid the dangers of annual climbing exploits.

An apple can be planted at any time between March and November when the soil is workable. Modern varieties are grafted onto rootstocks of different sizes. A semi-dwarf grafted onto an M9 rootstock is compact and easy to pick from, or you can choose one of the slim, upright and attractive 'Ballerina' types, which are even more manageable on a small plot.

Before planting, soak the roots in a bucket of water to which you have added a spadeful of compost and leave them for at least an hour. Dig a hole about 50 cm (20 in) deep and wide enough to accommodate the tree roots when well spread and add a little compost. Drive in a supporting stake alongside the hole, ideally covered with a plastic guard, then put in the tree with its 'neck' – the join between the top growth (the scion) and the rootstock – at least 7.5 cm (3 in) above the level of the soil. Fill in with soil and water well, then use a plastic or rubber tie to attach the tree firmly to the stake. It may help to add a watering spike alongside so that you can, if need be, water straight down to the roots. If you're planting more than one tree, allow a generous 4.5 m (15 ft) between them at least.

If conditions are favourable, and if your apple blossom has not been decimated by frost or wind, you will see clusters of apples beginning to form by late spring. Some will drop naturally, but if it is easy to get to the fruit they will benefit from being thinned out by hand. Use clean scissors or small secateurs to cut off any damaged, blemished or misshapen fruit and space the remainder to about 15 cm (6 in). Repeat the operation about two weeks later. Later, if any of the branches get too heavy, you may need to prop them up with some kind of forked support. You can use a piece of wood or some other device.

One branch had so many apples on it that it broke. (Robin Barrett)

If you improvise with your rake, be prepared to do without it for some weeks.

The table below gives a selection of allotment apple choices.

Self-fertile varieties

'Laxton's Fortune'	Eater; good acid balance	Prone to canker; harvest from September
'Queen Cox'	Eater; typical Cox taste and texture	Pick from late September
'Egremont Russet'	Sweet, nutty flavour	Mid season variety
'Braeburn'	Crisp and juicy	Mid to late season; keeps very well

Apples needing pollinators

'Worcester Pearmain'	Sweet, strawberry-flavoured flesh	Ripe from mid September, but not the best keeper
'Red Falstaff'	Heavy yields; stores well	Late-season variety
'Bramley'	Great-flavoured cooker with a fluffy texture; look for a vigorous small type such as 'Clone 20'	Needs two other group B pollinators

APPLE PROBLEMS

Our neighbour was rightly proud of her codling moth traps hanging on her Bramley – they worked really well for her. (Ruth)

Attack by the caterpillars (larvae) of the codling moth is the cause of maggoty apples with rotten insides. The moths lay their eggs in the young fruit, then the caterpillars feed from the inside as the fruit matures, making it drop prematurely. To help reduce attacks, buy a pheromone moth trap. Hang the open-sided box in the tree in early May; in its base you put a sticky sheet followed by a pheromone pellet. Because this pellet exudes a scent similar to that produced by virgin females, male moths are lured into the trap and get stuck, so the females are prevented from laying their eggs.

To help prevent more infestations, use string to tie strips of corrugated cardboard, smooth side outwards, around apple tree trunks in July. Well-fed larvae will crawl down the trunk and will be trapped inside, where they will hibernate. In early spring you can get rid of them by removing and burning the cardboard.

Canker is a disease that affects the bark of apple trees. Cracks with raised edges form in the branches from which a whitish gum may ooze. The best remedy is to cut away any affected branches and to cover the cuts with pine tar or a proprietary wound sealant to prevent further infection.

Plums and gages

These stone fruits are the stars of the allotment (gages are simply less hardy forms of plum). They are not too big, and are reasonably quick to mature – you should get fruit within three or four years. Even if they are not self-fertile, many plums pollinate easily, so you should be able to get a good crop from just one tree. Modern plums are grown on semi-dwarfing rootstocks so that trees are a reasonable size, even when mature. 'Pixie' rootstocks also have good resistance to the silver leaf infection, but are not everyone's choice.

I've come to the conclusion that small isn't beautiful when it comes to fruit. Orchard trees do better. The small ones get overloaded. (Simon Hewitt)

For your allotment plum, choose a sheltered spot that is going to suffer least from frost and wind. Like pears, plums fruit early and the blossom can be decimated by cold, windy spring weather. Autumn is the best time for planting – follow the same directions as for planting an apple (see p. 192) and keep it well watered. It will appreciate a mulch of compost in the first couple of years to help keep the roots moist, but after this it should only be fed every two or three years as overfeeding will stimulate it to produce stems and leaves rather than fruit. As the tree matures the only pruning you need do is to cut it back lightly to keep it in shape. Do this in late summer, before the tree enters its period of winter dormancy, to help avoid silver leaf infection.

It is important with plums to prevent branches laden with fruit from breaking, as wounds can be entry points for disease. Thinning a heavy crop is advisable, but should not be done before the end of June, after the tree has dropped excess fruit.

Hang weights on the branches to make them droop and expose more of the branch to sunlight. This results in more sap reaching the tips of the branches and better yields. (Tim Callard)

Silver leaf, a fungal infection that makes the leaves turn silver, is the most common problem with plums. When severe it also affects the bark, which may even have patches of the purple fungus on them. The best treatment is to cut away any affected branches and burn them; be sure to disinfect any tools you've used, to save spreading the spores. A very badly infected tree is best removed altogether. Codling moth caterpillars like plums as much as apples, so deter and trap them in the same way (see p. 193).

The following are the pick of plums and gages.

Plums

'Victoria'	Popular English plum; self-fertile	Harvest late August
'Czar'	Firm, purple-skinned; good pollinating partner with 'Victoria'	Harvest in early August
'Thames Cross'	Large, sweet; yellow-flushed fruit; late flowering so less prone to frost damage	Harvest mid to late September
'Marjorie's Seedling'	Late-flowering; deep purple fruit	Harvest from mid September

Gages

'Cambridge'	Yellow-green fruit; ideal pollinator is 'Marjorie's Seedling'	Harvest September
'Imperial Gage' (also sold as 'Denniston's Superb')	Self-fertile; green fruit; good for colder areas	Harvest mid August

Damsons

Close relations of plums, damsons are also easy to grow, but are not as sweet as plums or gages and unless absolutely ripe are best cooked or made into jam, jelly, chutney or a fruit syrup. 'Merryweather', the most easily available variety, is self-fertile and relatively quick to mature. A new tree should be planted in autumn and subsequently pruned, if necessary, in spring.

Pears

Most of the advice that applies to apples is also right for pears, though there are some differences. Pear trees do grow on allotments and, on old sites where trees are many decades old, can be huge. As with an apple, an existing pear is worth keeping as long as it is fruitful and reasonably healthy. However, you might want to think twice before planting a new pear since they take a long time to mature and are susceptible to wind. To avoid worrying about having nearby pollinators, a good choice for a new tree would be a self-fertile variety such as 'Concorde' grown on a dwarf rootstock. 'Conference' is partially self-fertile and has the advantage of being a very good keeper.

Pears can be variable, and may react badly to shade from other trees.

There's a 'Doyenne de Comice' under there and not a flower! But the 'Conference' does all right every year. (Reg Simmons)

The biggest problem with pears is pollination. Even if wind does not blow off the blossom before it has a chance to be fertilized, the wind may deter pollinating insects from reaching your tree. For this reason, if your plot is sheltered by a hedge or wall then you are likely to have more success with a pear than on an exposed site.

Pears will appreciate an annual mulch of good compost in early spring, as well as a thinning of any fruit you are able to reach during June.

CHAPTER 6
ALLOTMENT HARVEST

We eat something we've grown on the allotment almost every day of the year, even if it's just a spoonful of runner bean chutney or some raspberry jam. (Ruth)

Having an allotment makes you cook seasonally. (Pat Bence)

After all the efforts of digging, planting, weeding and watering comes the pleasurable task of harvesting your allotment crops, either to eat right away or to store for later. But don't believe that this is the end of your labours. When you find yourself making chutney or freezing fruit at midnight, or have more courgettes than you can possibly deal with, then you may the think that the harvest has got out of hand.

Allotment gluts can, however, be put to good use:

There is so much surplus on the allotment at this time of year we do a weekly trip to HARP, the local homeless refuge. (Ron Pankhurst)

When I was working I used to bundle up runner beans and take them into work and sell them. Then I donated the money to Médecins Sans Frontières. I did the same with courgettes. (Robin Barrett)

Once things start growing you'll need to keep an eye on crops like radishes so that you eat them before they get tough and woody. Some vegetables, such as purple sprouting broccoli, carry on growing the more you pick them and others like spinach can be prevented from running too quickly to seed by nipping out the tops as soon as they look to be making flower heads. If plants do go to seed then you may be able to save the heads either for flavouring (as with dill and fennel seeds) or for planting the following year.

'Big' crops like potatoes and onions that can't be left in the ground will need a place for storage and are not really the best choices if you don't have the facilities.

Harvesting can be a problem when you go on holiday.

My problem, to my great surprise, is getting people to pick things when I'm away. I did arrange with two neighbours to pick things and even gave them a key but I was distressed when I came back. I was staggered and saddened. (Edward Probert)

YOUR ALLOTMENT PRODUCE

The tips and suggestions in this chapter are just a few of the good ideas for harvesting and enjoying your allotment produce. Instructions for freezing and recipes for jams and chutneys can be found in good cookery books, but you'll always get the best flavour and freshness if you preserve fruit and vegetables when they are really fresh.

Plastic supermarket cartons are good for harvesting. Keep a stock of foil trays (bought or saved from take-aways) and hole-free plastic bags for freezing. If you like jam and chutney, save jars through the year so you have plenty to hand. For chutney and pickles you need lids with corrosion-resistant lid linings.

Vegetables

If you plan your allotment well there should be vegetables to harvest all year. If you do some of the preparation and trimming at the allotment you can throw all but the woodiest material on the compost heap. Apart from the specific preparations included in this chapter, be sure to trim and wash leafy vegetables well before you use them to get rid of any dirt as well as wildlife. The worst can be washed off at the plot if you have water handy.

You leave a bag of allotment vegetables on the kitchen floor and within the hour there are snails wandering around the floor. I throw them out onto the lawn and hope the birds will enjoy them, but often crush them first. (Ruth)

BROAD BEANS

It's essential to harvest these when young – they quickly get big and floury. Test a few pods for bean size before you pick them. On a summer's day it is a pleasure to sit in the sun and pod beans at the plot. They freeze excellently. When serving them fresh, you can do the purist thing and pop them out of their skins if you wish.

We always make sure we have enough allotment broad beans in the freezer to have at Christmas. They're a great reminder of summer. (Ruth)

The shoot tips, removed to discourage blackfly, are also edible:

If you nip out the tops they make a great vegetable for one meal – like broad bean flavoured spinach. They're a real delicacy if you cook them very lightly. (Chris Luck)

FRENCH BEANS

These need frequent picking to ensure you get them at their best. Dwarf French beans are very shallow rooted and it is easy to uproot plants accidentally as you pick. Using scissors to snip them off is a good move, or hold the plant with one hand while you nip off the stalk at the end of each bean with finger and thumb.

Helping my father pick French beans at his allotment I remember being reprimanded for pulling plants out of the ground. Ever since, I've always taken special care with them. (Ruth)

French beans, especially picked small, freeze reasonably well, and are fine for stir-fries. Lightly cooked they are good in salads (try them with tomatoes and basil) and essential for a *niçoise*. The purple ones turn a lovely dark green when cooked.

RUNNER BEANS

Runners need picking regularly, before they get stringy and 'beany'. If you miss some, take them off when you spot them and chuck them in the compost or leave them and keep the seeds for next year. Larger ones will need their sides 'stringing' before they are sliced and cooked. They freeze well, even without blanching, and make excellent chutney with onions, sugar, turmeric and chilli. They are also successful in stir-fries and even curries.

> *My mother always put her runners through a mechanical slicer. I favour cutting them slightly larger, by hand, which I think preserves their structure and flavour much better. (Ruth)*

BORLOTTI AND HARICOT BEANS

These need to be left on the plants until the pods are crisp and dry, which will probably be September or October. Pick them on a dry day and put them in the sun or a warm place until the pods are crisp, then shell them and spread them on trays to dry completely. Store them in airtight jars.

PEAS

Of all allotment vegetables, peas freeze best of all. Pick peas when the pods feel firm and full – but not hard and floury – which may be daily. Test them by popping a few. Any that do go over can be left, then be harvested and dried like haricots. Watch out for any grubs in the pods.

MANGETOUTS

Unlike ordinary peas, mangetouts do not freeze well at all, which is why it is best to plant them in succession so you are not overloaded, although they will keep in the fridge for up to a week. Because they can turn almost overnight from tiny to oversized pods they need to be picked regularly. You can leave any big ones to develop, then shell them, but you are unlikely to get a worthwhile crop. Cook and serve mangetouts as you would ordinary peas. Lightly cooked and cooled, and with sun-dried tomatoes, feta cheese and mint, they make a great salad.

We tried freezing our first ever crop of allotment mangetouts with disappointing results, so we didn't bother again. Now we just give away any surpluses. (Ruth)

Brassicas

When you harvest brassicas, compost the leaves. Because the stems can take years to rot, either burn them, put them in the next skip your site provides or take them to your local recycling centre.

CABBAGE

Most modern cabbages stand reasonably well, but you need to pick and eat them before the heads 'blow' (and even flower) or before they get mushy on the outside and riddled with snails and slugs.

Any good cabbage will have a firm head, and even one that is past its best can probably be used if you cut off all the outside leaves. If you don't need to clear the ground immediately, try cutting off cabbage heads with a sharp knife and leaving the stumps in place. Small clumps of leaves should sprout from these, which can be picked and eaten.

Crisp white or pale cabbage, and tender red cabbage, is great eaten cooked or raw, but the darker green varieties are better cooked. Cabbage can also be pickled or fermented into sauerkraut.

I freeze red cabbage casseroled with onions, garlic, apples and red wine and some strips of orange zest added for extra flavour. (Ruth)

KALE

To enjoy kale at its most tender, take out the central heart first of all as this will encourage the growth of new side shoots. It can be used like any dark green cabbage, but needs to be finely chopped to be palatable. Very finely shredded deep-fried kale is the 'seaweed' served topped with brown sugar in Chinese restaurants, and easy to make at home.

BRUSSELS SPROUTS

It is said that frost improves the flavour of sprouts, which is fine if they are a frost-resistant variety, but otherwise it will make them mushy. Pick sprouts from the bottom of the stem, taking them from a few plants each time. Before and as you pick, remove any yellowing leaves. At the end of the season cut off and eat the head – a bonus when there are few fresh vegetables to harvest. With luck the last few sprouts will swell some more.

Cooked sprouts, the obligatory accompaniment to the Christmas turkey, are not everyone's favourite and are almost universally loathed by children. Sprout lovers relish them with bacon and garlic, or with roast chestnuts, or in a soup flavoured with nutmeg. Small, tight, blanched sprouts will freeze well.

Salad surprise: a mixture of raw, finely sliced sprouts mixed with grated carrot, chopped dates and walnuts mixed in a dressing made with a mixture of equal quantities of mayonnaise and low fat crème fraîche and with a dash of orange juice. (Ruth)

SPROUTING BROCCOLI

Said to be the poor man's asparagus, sprouting broccoli needs picking little and often – with your fingers or ideally with the help of a knife – and the more you pick the more you get. It is delicious steamed or boiled and served hot or cold. It is best eaten fresh as it doesn't freeze well.

CALABRESE (BROCCOLI)

If you cut the heads of calabrese and leave plants intact, side shoots and extra small heads will, with luck, be produced around the top of the stem. Heads are best sliced off with a knife. Calabrese is versatile, though best parboiled before being added to stir-fries or used in a salad. Try it in vegetable curry or cooked *au gratin* like cauliflower.

CAULIFLOWER

As your cauliflowers mature, begin harvesting them when they are quite small. If you leave them you will have a glut, though they will keep for a week or two if hung upside down in a cool place and sprayed daily with cold water. Use a sharp knife to cut off each head, including a good number of protective leaves.

Use cauliflower as you would calabrese; for salads it needs to be a little cooked before being cooled and dressed.

My favourite cauliflower curry: fry garlic, onions, a chopped chilli, some mustard seeds and garam masala in groundnut oil. Add parboiled cauliflower, coconut milk, salt and pepper and cook until the cauliflower is tender. (Ruth)

SPINACH

Leaves of spinach need picking little and often if you can. Cooked spinach freezes well.

I've found that one good way of preventing it seeding too quickly is to pick any central shoots that look as if they are about to bolt. (Ruth)

Small, tender spinach leaves are excellent in salads. When cooking spinach there is no need to add any additional water if you start it on a low heat. Before serving plain it needs pressing in a colander with a saucer or small plate. A mixture of spinach and butter puréed in a blender makes a quick sauce for pasta or meat balls. Spinach can be added direct to a stir-fry or curry. Cooked spinach can be added to a quiche or will make a salad with a dressing of olive oil, mustard and lemon juice.

SWISS CHARD

Like spinach, chard is best picked young, before it has a chance for the leaves to get bitter and the stems stringy. The leaves can be used like spinach, and pack a stronger flavour. The stems can be cooked and served whole, either plain or with a sauce, or chopped and added to any vegetable dish.

We experimented with Swiss chard and decided we liked the stems much better than the leaves. (Ruth)

PAK CHOI AND MIZUNA

When very small these are great picked and eaten raw. When bigger they are ideal for stir-fries. Small hearty pak choi can be parboiled then braised in the oven. Neither is at all good frozen.

GLOBE ARTICHOKES

When they are full but firm, cut off large globes with a knife or secateurs, beginning with the topmost or 'king' head. As you do so, take the opportunity to strengthen the plant by cutting back each stem to about half its original length.

If you miss some and they flower, cut off the whole stems and use them indoors as eye-catching flower arrangements. (Ruth)

Before you cook globe artichokes, trim the stems level with the base. If you wish you can snip the tips off the leafy flower scales, too. Then boil them in water with some lemon juice added to prevent discolouration. Test that they are done by pulling away one of the outermost scales – it should come away easily. Otherwise, pull apart the topmost ones and pull out both the small inner scales, followed by the hairy choke, for which you will need the help of a spoon. Serve them with a vinaigrette. Cooked chokes can be cooled and preserved in olive oil.

ASPARAGUS

To harvest asparagus you need a sharp knife so that you can cut off spears below ground level. This helps reduce the asparagus aroma so attractive to asparagus beetles. By tradition, you should stop harvesting asparagus on the longest day – 21 June – but whatever variety you are growing you should only carry on cutting for six to eight weeks. Cut spears regularly and don't worry if you miss some. Just let them grow naturally into their 'ferns' which, after the harvest is over, need to be allowed to grow for the rest of the summer. If you have a few spears and need more to make a meal, put them in iced water for a few hours, then wrap them in kitchen paper, put them into a plastic bag and refrigerate them until you need them.

There is no need to cut an asparagus spear once it's been harvested. I've found that if you bend it gently it will snap at the point where the woodier base begins. The ends are great for asparagus or any vegetable stock or soup. (Ruth)

Asparagus can be steamed, grilled or boiled. Big spears can be cooked upright in a pan part filled with water so that the tips steam and the bases boil. Served simply with butter, hollandaise or vinaigrette, they are delicious. You can also cook and add them to quiches and they freeze quite well after super-quick blanching.

CELERY

To prevent damage, celery is best lifted with a fork. You will need to harvest self-blanching sorts before they get damaged by frost. Keep the green tops to use as herbs or add them to the stockpot. If you have more celery than you can use, freeze it after cooking (for instance braised or made into soup).

For party canapés, fill celery with softened cream cheese or smoked salmon pâté, then cut them into bite-sized lengths. (Ruth)

FLORENCE FENNEL

Fennel can be used much as celery, and is an even better match with fish. Trim the roots off the plants as you lift them and cut back the tops, keeping some to use late in the season when the herb fennel is over.

Chopped cooked fennel, added with cooked onions to smoked haddock in a cheese sauce and browned under the grill after being generously topped with breadcrumbs, is a superb supper dish. (Ruth)

RADISHES

Pull your radishes regularly – initially to thin a row – and eat them young. Big winter radishes can be left in the ground until you need them or harvested and stored in a box in a cool dark place. They are best grated or very finely sliced. They are perfect just dipped in salt as a pre-dinner treat.

BEETROOT

The beetroot crop begins with adding the leaves of thinnings to salads – like spinach they mix brilliantly with bacon and avocado. Roots can then be lifted and used as you need them. If you have some left in the ground in autumn, either pull them up and use them for pickles or secure some fleece over them as frost protection. Alternatively, pull them and store them in a box of peat in a cool dark place.

To prevent the beetroot bleeding, and to help preserve their flavour, wash them well, then boil, bake or microwave them in their skins. (If microwaving, wrap them individually in cling film and turn them several times during cooking.)

Another good cooking method is to:

Peel and chop big beetroot into 25-mm (1-inch) cubes, put in a bowl with a few tablespoons of water, cover and microwave on high for 5 minutes. Stir and repeat once or twice until tender, then drain. (Ruth)

Alternatively, peel and chop them and bake them in foil with oil and chopped red onions added. Or make borsch to serve hot or cold, adding either lemon juice or a can of tomatoes to prevent the soup being too sweet.

Tiny, tender beetroot are delicious boiled and served with a mustard and mayonnaise dressing. Beetroot 'coleslaw', made by tossing raw, grated beetroot in a mixture of French dressing, mayonnaise, yoghurt and horseradish is surprisingly tasty. (Ruth)

CARROTS
Use a fork to make carrots easier to lift, then trim the tops. The crop can be left in the ground (cover with fleece to protect it from frost). Alternatively, if you have a cool dark space suitable for storage (if this is in your shed, it should be protected from rodents), lift and trim them, check for soundness and pack them in boxes of sand. Be selective; black indentations and tunnels made by carrot fly attack can be hard to spot until you actually scrape or peel them.

Carrots are hugely versatile, both raw and cooked. If you have a freezer big enough, they can be blanched and frozen.

Carrot cake, made with fresh allotment carrots, is one of life's luxuries. (Ruth)

CELERIAC
Unless you can be sure of protecting it from frost damage, celeriac needs to be eaten before the ground becomes icy, or lifted in November and stored in sand, as for carrots. It also freezes well if pre-cooked. However, the roots will carry on swelling right through the autumn.

Because the flesh quickly discolours on contact with air, celeriac benefits from being put into water with lemon juice added as you peel and chop it. It is excellent grated and eaten raw, roasted or boiled and mashed, either on its own or with potato.

Add some simply cooked fish and a rasher or two of bacon to mashed celeriac and you have a feast. (Ruth)

PARSNIPS

As soon as their foliage begins to fade, parsnips are ready to lift with a fork. They are usually frost hardy so can be left in the ground all winter. In spring, any parsnips you haven't eaten will start to sprout green tops again. By this stage they are usually very woody but if you cut out the cores they are fine to eat.

When we need to clear the ground in spring we dig up the last of the parsnips, trim and cook them then freeze them; they are a great stand-by. (Ruth)

Parsnips are excellent roasted or boiled and mashed, and are good in casseroles. Curried parsnip soup is highly recommended.

TURNIPS

To prevent them getting woody and over pungent, turnips need lifting regularly – ideally they should get no larger than tennis balls. Winter turnips can be left until you need them. Summer ones, essential ingredients of a *navarin* of lamb, can be peeled, blanched and frozen.

KOHL RABI

Like turnips, these are best pulled and eaten when small and tender, but are excellent raw – and with the benefit of a milder flavour.

SWEDES

Totally frost tolerant, swedes are the archetypal winter vegetable. Use a fork to lift them as you need them. You can pull them in October when they are still quite small, and store them in a cool place in your shed or garage (though be careful to protect them from hungry rodents). They can be tough to peel and cut. Boiled and mashed with plenty of butter and pepper they are the 'neeps' which make a traditional accompaniment to haggis.

POTATOES

Even if you are not growing earlies you may want to harvest some main crops as 'new' potatoes. If so, they should be dug when they are about the size of hens' eggs. You can test whether they're ready by using your hands to push the soil away from a plant at the end of a row.

> *For a main crop, test the skin before you lift them. If it scrapes off easily when rubbed with your thumb, then it is ready. (Ruth)*

When digging or lifting potatoes you need to be careful not to spike them. Try to insert the fork at least 15 cm (6 in) away from the stem. As you pick the potatoes out of the ground (a companion is invaluable for this task) check that any potatoes you want to keep long term are undamaged, either by the fork or by wireworms. Discard at once any that are green. If the soil and crop are wet, you may want to leave them on the soil surface for a day or two to dry out. Go back along the row, too, to make sure you have got all the potatoes out. However hard you try it may well seem impossible to avoid tiny potatoes springing up as 'volunteers' the following year.

> *If you are helping to pick potatoes, mind where you put your feet. When I was a child my father accidentally pierced my boot – and my foot. It needed a trip to casualty but no stitches. (Ruth)*

Traditionally, sound potatoes are stored in 'breathable' hessian sacks and kept in a dark, cool place. For many people this is not going to be possible, and a sack kept in the shed is likely to be quickly eaten by hungry rodents. But there is an alternative.

> *For many years we kept potatoes very successfully in a galvanized metal dustbin in the shed. We packed them in layers, with newspaper in between, and they kept for months. It also meant that we had good reasons to visit the allotment all through the winter. (Ruth)*

SWEET POTATOES

Because they don't keep well, sweet potatoes need to be eaten before the end of the season. Cooked, they will freeze well if you have the space.

JERUSALEM ARTICHOKES

These hardy tubers will survive right through the winter in the ground. As with potatoes, it is worth the effort to pick out all the minute tubers, which will readily sprout again. As a vegetable, artichokes can be used in all the same ways as other root vegetables. Artichoke soup is an all-time favourite.

ONIONS

No good cook will ever be without onions, the essential flavouring for so many dishes, and will welcome small as well as mammoth allotment offerings. For eating uncooked, spring and red onions have by far the mildest flavour.

When onions are nearly ready to be harvested the leaves begin to turn yellow. At this point you should bend over the tops and leave them for a couple of weeks. Then, ideally in a dry, sunny spell, dig or gently pull them up and leave them upside down to ripen off for about a week. Do not be tempted to cut off the tops before they have died back properly or you may encourage the entry of rot. If the weather is wet you may need to put the ripening onions in your shed or even take them home and put them in the garage or a spare room.

By lucky chance we inherited three rusty but sturdy large wire mesh 'trays' about 10 cm (4 in) deep. Turned upside down they were the perfect place to put onions and garlic for ripening and, if it rained, could simply be carried into the shed. (Ruth)

If you are going away in August, then ingenuity can pay off:

We always go away in the first week of August so, a couple of weeks before, I 'break' the roots by turning over the tops. Then just before we leave I put them, bottoms up, on seed trays, facing south and with cloches over the top for the three or four weeks we're away. That gets them baked hot and in September I hang them. We've even had onions to take away the following August. (Chris Luck)

Make a loop of twine. Wrap two onion ends together, tie them around the twine and pull them down to the bottom. Continue until you have a whole string. (Tim Pryce)

Or you can use string bags and hang them when full in a cool, dry place away from direct sunlight.

SPRING ONIONS

Lift spring onions with a fork as you need them – if growing close together they may break off if you pull them with your hands. Midsummer plantings will last right through until spring. Any that go to flower can be used like garden alliums for decoration.

SHALLOTS

After pulling, shallots need to be separated out, left for a few days to ripen in the sun, then hung up in a net in a cool place for the winter. To make them easier to peel and prepare, a good trick is to immerse them in boiling water for a few minutes. They pack a real punch as pickled onions or an ingredient of piccallilli.

GARLIC

Unless you are growing the variety 'Mediterranean', which makes flower stems as part of its normal growth (and needs cutting back two or three weeks before lifting), garlic is best harvested before it runs to flower. You will certainly want to use some fresh or 'wet', for its superbly mild flavour. Whole heads are deliciously mild when roasted.

For the bulk of the crop, which you will want to store, lift it gently with a fork – ideally when the weather forecast predicts a few days of dry weather – and leave it out in the open to ripen. When dry, it can be strung up and kept in your shed (as long as it is waterproof) or in a cool spot at home.

In London, where there was little room for storage, I tied my allotment garlic to a piece of strong string and hung them alongside the kitchen window. It kept all winter – and enhanced the view. (Ruth)

LEEKS

You can begin lifting leeks (use a fork) when they are small and tender. The tops and roots can be trimmed off at the plot and put in the compost. They last all winter, and will continue growing slowly right through until late spring, although by that time the centres are likely to be woody. If you want to clear the ground, any excess will freeze well, cooked, and they are useful in summer, before the next crop is ready, for making vichyssoise.

Leeks always need loads of washing; dirt and grit cling to them with limpet-like force. (Ruth)

If you want to use leeks whole, make two cuts, at right angles, down the centre of each and wash them under running water.

COURGETTES

Round ones like 'Eight Ball' are lovely. I just take the tops off and scoop them out and stuff them. (Maureen Nightingale)

Ask almost any allotment courgette grower and they will complain of excesses. And how is it that small ones manage to explode into 'marrows' overnight? Picking courgettes regularly will help and you can always cook the flowers, in batter, Italian style. Once you've cropped them (ideally, with a knife to prevent the tops breaking), big ones will keep several weeks in a cool dark place. Because of their high water content, the best way to freeze them is in tomato sauce or as a ratatouille, or puréed as a basis for soups.

Here are some other personal solutions for the courgette mountain:

• *Sliced crosswise and sautéed in olive oil with basil or tarragon (and garlic), or with lemon juice and pesto;*
• *Sliced lengthwise, brushed with oil and grilled or baked (for the latter, add peppers, squash, tomatoes). Good hot or cold. Add herbs and flavourings as you wish;*
• *Courgette, cheese and mushroom quiche;*
• *Courgette and onion frittata (and with bacon or chicken added for meat eaters);*
• *Stuffed courgette (scooped out, microwaved for 5 minutes, stuffed and baked for 45 minutes). Stuffing mixture can be meat and/or vegetables and nuts, with rice, breadcrumbs etc.;*
• *Courgette soup – with onions, lemon and herbs such as tarragon, topped with yoghurt (also excellent cold);*
• *Courgette and potato gratin;*

- *Courgette ribbon salad (sliced into thin ribbons lengthwise with a wide vegetable peeler and dressed). You can then add any other ingredients you like – try anchovies, capers, preserved lemons or chopped gherkins for some 'bite';*
- *Courgette couscous – with herbs and, if you like, garlic and/or onions, tomatoes;*
- *Courgette pancakes – grated courgettes mixed with Scotch pancake batter and fried;*
- *Courgette* niçoise *– substitute cooked or raw courgettes for green beans in this classic salad.*

> *Last but not least, the flowers can be picked and fried, Italian style, which can help reduce the quantity of vegetables. A ricotta stuffing is excellent. (Ruth)*

And possibly something to avoid:

> *An American friend persuaded me to make a chocolate and courgette cake – it was foul! (Vicky Scott)*

MARROWS

Marrows need cutting with a knife. If you have spare marrows at the end of the season, they will keep well in a cool garage, ideally strung in individual nets. They are excellent halved lengthwise, scooped out and stuffed, or the flesh can be cubed and baked. Spaghetti marrows are best baked whole and the cooked flesh spooned out and used like pasta.

SQUASHES AND PUMPKINS

> *I pick them early so they don't get too big. (Vicky Scott)*

These are ready to harvest if, when tapped, they give a slightly hollow sound. Thanks to their thick skins, both will keep all winter in a cool dark place. Just peel, cut into chunks and use. For pumpkin pie the flesh needs to be puréed, sieved and cooled before use.

> *I thought I had used all the squashes then in April I discovered two more in the back of the cupboard. They were still perfect. (Ruth)*

TOMATOES

Allotment tomatoes have the best flavour when picked fully ripe, but if, as autumn approaches, you still have lots of green fruit, don't discard them. Green tomatoes are excellent stir-fried, or as a classic chutney ingredient. You may also be able to persuade them to ripen by putting them in a basket in an airing cupboard. They can also be individually wrapped in tissue paper and put in a drawer or a cardboard box. That way you may have home-grown fruit right into November.

> Put your green tomatoes in a drawer with a ripe banana; the gasses given off will help ripen them. (Tim Callard)

There are other ways, too:

> The last weekend in September I cut off all the trusses from my tomatoes and put them in a 2 ft 6 in square propagator lined with perlite, which is not needed at that time of year. I put in all my tomatoes and had the last ones in February that way. (Chris Luck)

It is always handy to have a stock of tomato sauce or purée in the freezer and worth the trouble of peeling the tomatoes first. Pouring boiling water over them will split the skins to make the job easier.

CUCUMBERS AND GHERKINS

Outdoor cucumbers are best picked when small, before they have a chance to get bitter, but even these need peeling before they are eaten. Big ones will also need their seeds scooping out. Excesses will freeze well as a soup (to serve cold) made by puréeing cucumbers with light stock, spring onions, mint and yoghurt. They are also good in chutneys and pickles. Pick gherkins regularly as they mature and use them for pickles. Add heads of dill flowers for an authentic flavour.

PEPPERS

Peppers are green when unripe, then ripen to red, yellow or purple, depending on variety, but can be picked and eaten at any stage. They are ideal for stir-fries and baking (with stuffing if you wish). For freezing they are best added to a dish such as ratatouille.

CHILLIES

Like peppers, chillies turn colour as they ripen and can be picked at any stage. The bulk of the crop can be dried and stored in airtight jars (remember their fieriness increases with drying) or chopped and mixed with olive oil.

> *By mid September one year we had already picked dozens of chillies and the rest we dried in the airing cupboard. They kept in an airtight jar for two years and were still very potent. (Ruth)*

AUBERGINES

Ripe aubergines are either a glossy purple or a pale creamy colour and can be roasted, fried or added to dishes such as ratatouille. Blanched and sliced they will freeze reasonably well.

SWEETCORN

Just pull apart the leafy sheath around a cob and press a nail into one of the seeds, which should be plump and pale yellow. If it exudes a creamy liquid, then it is ready to pick and eat or freeze. They freeze excellently, either on or off their cobs. To remove the kernels, hold the cob upright then use a sharp knife to cut downwards, near the core of each cob. A fresh cob, boiled and served with butter, salt and pepper is one of the delights of late summer.

Salad leaves

The way you harvest your salads depends on what you're growing, but many can be picked as handfuls or bags of leaves until the plants are spent or go to seed. All are best eaten as fresh as possible, but because they are so fresh will keep for several days in the fridge. All need washing well to get rid of any dirt and unwelcome wildlife.

LETTUCE

Small, hearty lettuces like Little Gem are pulled up and eaten whole, but you can pick the leaves of loose-leafed varieties as required. When you have a glut (which is almost inevitable) try braised lettuce as a vegetable accompaniment.

Shredded lettuce, added with butter to peas or mangetouts with some chopped spring onions, makes peas in the French style. A family favourite. (Ruth)

ROCKET AND SORREL

Pick leaf by leaf. Best in salad mixed with less stringent ingredients such as lettuce and avocado.

RADICCHIO

Radicchio is worth protecting with fleece when it's frosty, but is a good winter stand-by and will last through until April.

After a frost, a bed of radicchio looked soggy and brown. But having pulled up a couple of plants and removed what remained of the outer leaves, bright purple hearts, perfectly edible, were revealed inside. (Ruth)

CORN SALAD

It is fiddly to pick off individual leaves of this crop, so you may prefer to harvest plants whole and just trim off the roots once a good rosette of leaves has formed.

LAND CRESS

Also fiddly to pick – and needs plenty of washing, especially if leaves have been in contact with the soil.

HERBS AND FLOWERS

Herbs

All allotment herbs can be used fresh as you need them. Those with soft leaves will keep their flavour chopped and frozen in ice cube trays. Unless you are growing for seed, harvest herbs you plan to freeze or dry just before they flower, when their flavour will be most intense.

Ideal for this treatment are: parsley, dill, fennel, tarragon, chervil, mint and lovage. Bay leaves, packed in plastic pots, also freeze well and are handy if you don't get to the allotment often in winter.

Many herbs can also be cut, hung in a warm dry place, dried and stored in airtight jars. Good for this treatment are: sage, tarragon, thyme, rosemary and marjoram (oregano). Many of these are good to add to pot-pourris as well as to food.

FOR SAUCES AND JELLIES

If you want to make mint sauce for keeping, or mint jelly, the best time to harvest the leaves is just before the plants come into flower, as this is when their flavour is most concentrated.

Every other year, before it goes to flower, I pick as much mint as I can find (just the ordinary spearmint) and make a big jar of mint sauce by chopping it, boiling it with vinegar and sugar and ladling it into screw-top jars. It lasts and lasts — and matures in flavour. (Ruth)

HERB BUTTERS AND OILS

Any fresh herbs mashed into butter or added as whole sprigs to olive oil make versatile ingredients. Herb butters freeze remarkably well, too. If you want to add garlic this is best done after defrosting.

SEEDS

For seeds to flavour curries and other spicy dishes it is worth letting some herbs go to seed. Pick and dry the heads, then shake out the seeds into a bag before storing them in airtight jars. Best herbs for seeds are coriander, fennel and dill.

HORSERADISH

You will need a strong fork or spade to dig up horseradish. In late autumn a good ploy is to lift and store roots in boxes of peat through the winter. From these will come the roots to start off next year's crop. In the kitchen horseradish needs to be peeled and grated. It is best used fresh, but can be preserved in white vinegar if you wish.

Flowers

The seeds of some flowers can be harvested and eaten.

NASTURTIUM SEEDS

Ripe seeds allowed to dry out thoroughly for a couple of days can be sprinkled with salt then pickled in flavoured vinegar – they taste like capers.

SUNFLOWERS

Once seeds have formed, be sure to get to them before the birds if you want to enjoy them yourself or collect them to put in bird feeders. An easy way of harvesting them is to enclose the heads in a piece of muslin, or pick them when the seeds are formed but not yet ripe and dry them indoors.

FRUIT

Soft fruit

All soft fruit can be frozen – either in bags or put on trays to open-freeze first. Even if it doesn't keep its texture the flavour is unsurpassed. Soft fruit also makes great jam and ice cream and is the basis for desserts such as mousses and fools, pies and crumbles.

STRAWBERRIES

If you can't get to your allotment every day, it is worth picking strawberries just as they are beginning to ripen and finishing them off indoors. You may not get 100 per cent good fruit, but it's better than the disappointment of seeing them rotting on the plants. Frozen, defrosted strawberries have a horrible texture but puréed make a superb sauce (cold or hot) to accompany everything from ice cream to a chocolate torte.

RASPBERRIES, LOGANBERRIES AND HYBRID FRUIT

A raspberry crop will need picking every few days. If rain has made the fruit soggy it can be picked and puréed or discarded, depending on its condition. Raspberries keep their texture much better than strawberries when frozen and defrosted.

I pick them [raspberries] every two days to stop any mould spreading. (Edward Probert)

A summer pudding made with frozen allotment raspberries and redcurrants is our traditional family dessert on New Year's Eve. (Ruth)

Loganberries, boysenberries and tayberries all have an even firmer texture than raspberries, and freeze better.

GOOSEBERRIES
Even if you need the nimbleness of bare hands for fruit picking, protect your arms with long sleeves when you harvest your gooseberries. Topped and tailed they freeze very well – a perfect crumble or fool ingredient. To take the edge off their tartness, mix them with apples.

BLACKCURRANTS
It is rare for all the currants on one sprig to ripen simultaneously, so you will have to spend time picking the first of them as they ripen. Later, you should get whole sprigs – use a fork to remove or 'strig' them without damaging the fruit – a good job to do on the plot on a sunny day.

RED AND WHITE CURRANTS
When really ripe, redcurrants are a deep crimson. Because they are even more fiddly to harvest than blackcurrants, it is worth waiting until you have sprigs in which all the fruit are more or less mature, even if you have to discard a few unripe ones from the ends. They can then be strigged like blackcurrants, though for redcurrant jelly this is unnecessary. Ripe white currants are actually a pale cream colour. It's always exciting to have clear jars of redcurrant jelly lined up.

I've got one bush and last year I left what I didn't need. They stay on the bush for months. It was late September or October before I picked them. They just get a darker and darker red. (Edward Probert)

BLACKBERRIES

Unless you have thornless ones, pick blackberries with care. They freeze well, keeping their texture and flavour. With apples they make one of the best jellies.

BLUEBERRIES

Also great for freezing – and jam – if the birds don't get them first.

CAPE GOOSEBERRIES

Left in their husks, cape gooseberries will keep for several weeks. If not eaten raw they are best used for jam.

RHUBARB

From spring onwards, pull and trim rhubarb as you need it; the poisonous leaves can safely go into the compost heap or bin. By July or August it will be stringy and past its best. Rhubarb freezes well either chopped and raw or cooked.

A favourite crumble is rhubarb mixed with chopped stem ginger or grated orange zest, and with cinnamon, ground ginger and almonds added to the topping. (Ruth)

Tree Fruit

On the allotment, the biggest problem with harvesting tree fruit can be getting to the crop before it falls to the ground. Windfalls can be used as long as they have not decayed or been eaten by birds or insects. Chuck the worst into the compost.

APPLES

You are bound to get windfall apples, which can be picked up and, if not too decayed, cut up and eaten at once, either raw in a fruit salad or cooked. For good keeping you need perfect, unbruised fruit picked by hand. A perfectly ripe apple will, ideally, come away easily when you put a hand under it and twist a little.

Failing an apple harvester we developed a two-person act: one up the tree, the other catching fruit as they were thrown down. Undoubtedly breaking all the rules of health and safety, but hugely satisfying when we had all the fruit in the bag. (Ruth)

To make harvesting from high branches easier it helps to have some kind of apple picker. Garden centres now sell these, which consist of a bag attached to a circle of prongs at the end of a long handle. The prongs are pressed against the fruit stems and the fruit falls into the bag. Once you have all your apples, make sure they are clean and dry then either store them stalk downwards in cardboard trays so that they do not touch, or wrap them individually in newspaper. Keep an eye on them over the winter and get rid of any rotters before they spread their germs to their neighbours.

One of the most satisfying things is picking apples for storage. We have eaten apples right through until May. They're perfect with a piece of cheese. (Mike Cosgrove)

Apples can be frozen cooked and puréed or simply peeled, chopped and bagged up mixed with a little sugar. They keep their taste and texture well.

Apple slices or rings, dipped in a mixture of lemon juice and water, can be dried overnight in a very low oven, cooled and stored in airtight jars.

PLUMS, GAGES AND DAMSONS
Plums freeze well (ideally, halved and stoned) either raw or cooked, but they do need to be picked before they fall off the trees and before the wasps can get to them. All are good for jam and chutney. Plums can also be added to the mixture to make a superb fruity Bakewell tart.

PEARS
Pears need to be picked during autumn before they are ripe, and stored in a cool, dark place until they are ready to eat – and tall trees will present the same challenges as apples. Once the flesh near the stalk begins to soften they can be brought into a warm room to finish ripening for a couple of days.

Like apples, pears can be oven-dried and make an excellent snack or addition to cereals.

INDEX